THE COLD WAR

THE COLD WAR
by Deane and Dave Heller

Illustrated with photographs

Hawthorn Books, Inc.

Publishers

New York

To David

CONTENTS

Chapter One

THE SEEDS
OF THE COLD WAR
ARE SOWN

"The Russians are running all of Berlin."
—Col. Frank Howley,
Berlin, July, 1945

From the holocaust that was Berlin on April 30, 1945, with its Nazi government center reduced to ruins; from the jagged shells of bombed-out buildings standing in mute testimony to the horrors of war; from piles of rubble and thick, black clouds of smoke rising hundreds of feet skyward came a whispered rumor soon to sweep the world—HITLER DEAD!

On this historic day, the fierce battle for the Nazi capital neared its final hours. Russian tanks reached points only one-half mile from the Führer's underground fortified bunker beneath the Nazi headquarters. In the bunker, an eerie sort of life was still going on. The survivors of the Nazi inner circle were making frantic, last-minute plans. For most there seemed to be only two choices—escape or death.

Hitler and his wife, the former Eva Braun, chose death. Later, Colonel Otto Gunsche, who entered their private rooms, gave a report of what had happened. Hitler, the Colonel said, had shot himself and Eva had poisoned herself with cyanide. The bodies were then wrapped in blankets, doused with gasoline, and burned. Later Soviet evidence, based on tests performed on the charred bodies, indicates that Hitler also took cyanide, and that Hitler's valet, Heinz Linge, fired the gun after the dictator's death.

Dr. Joseph Goebbels, the Reich Propaganda Minister, and his

wife, Magda, also chose death—for themselves and their six children. Helga, Holde, Hilde, Heide, Hedda, and Helmuth were given poison while they slept. Others, like Martin Bormann and Colonel Gunsche escaped into the chaos of embattled Berlin after Hitler's suicide.

Only a few squares away from Hitler's bunker, a ferocious street battle was going on. Fanatical Nazi troops under General Karl Weidling struggled in combat with the Russian Eighth Guards Army of Colonel General Vasili Chuikov. Ground was yielded building by building. The dreaded S.S. troops scoured the inner city for Nazi deserters, forcing them to fight. "Fight or die!" was the order. Many German soldiers who sought to escape were shot by the S.S. Russian artillery fire battered the city. A Swiss correspondent in Berlin during the battle estimated that artillery shells landed every five seconds.

Berlin on the final day of April, 1945, was a city of death. The death toll was staggering; the number of Russian and Nazi soldiers and German civilians who died has been estimated as high as 250,000. Nobody really knows, for during the battle there was no time to count. Bodies lay in heaps along the impassable, ruined streets, which were pitted with bomb craters. Bodies littered the Reichstag Building, where hard-core Nazi storm troopers had barricaded themselves, vowing to fight to the last man.

On the western outskirts of the city, streams of German refugees on foot and on bicycles, some with their possessions piled in horse-drawn wagons, clogged the roads. Russian planes strafed and artillery fire often raked the columns of people fleeing the Reich capital. The last Western air raid on Berlin, the 363rd of the war, had ended on April 21, as the ground battle for the city had begun. Now the heavy artillery, with its deafening scream, and shrapnel from the exploding shells spread terrifying destruction.

The first non-German to learn of Hitler's death was Colonel General Vasili Ivanovich Chuikov. His informant was Lieutenant General Hans Krebs, Hitler's Chief of the Army General Staff, who contacted the Russians and tried to surrender—on conditions that were refused. It was the Allies first certain news that Hitler had chosen to stay—and die—in Berlin rather than barricading himself into his "Eagle's Nest" stronghold at Berchtesgaden as they had expected.

Hitler's death and the collapse of the Nazi armies electrified the world. On May 2, *The New York Times* carried three eight-column banner headlines:

Hitler Dead in Chancellery, Nazis Say:
Doenitz, Successor, Orders War To Go On:
Berlin Almost Won: U.S. Armies Advance

The *Times* also reported that, in New York City, the news of Hitler's death brought rush-hour subway traffic to a standstill as thousands stopped to buy newspapers and read the reports of his death. But in Washington, D.C., Harry S. Truman, who had recently become President of the United States on the death of Franklin D. Roosevelt, urged people not to celebrate the coming victory in Europe. President Truman solemnly said: "Americans should dedicate themselves to the task ahead." The task, of course, was the still unfinished war with the Japanese.

In Moscow, Joseph Stalin hailed the raising of the Soviet flag over the Brandenberg Gate, Berlin's best-known landmark. In southwest Germany, American troops captured the infamous Dachau concentration camp and were sickened by the sight of 32,000 living skeletons imprisoned there. From Milan, Italy, came photos of the dead Italian dictator, Benito Mussolini, who had been executed by Italian partisans and hung by the heels in the main public square.

The world news swept on at a breathtaking pace. On May 4, 1945, the headlines in the *Times* were jubilant:

The War In Europe Ended!
Surrender Is Unconditional:
V-E Will Be Proclaimed Today
Our Troops In Okinawa Gain

At Rheims, France, in the little red schoolhouse that was used as a headquarters by General of the Allied Armies Dwight D. Eisenhower, he and Nazi General Alfred Jodl had placed their signatures on the unconditional surrender documents.

All over the world, people rejoiced that there was to be peace in Europe. "London Delirious in V-E Carnival" and "Millions Rejoice in V-E Celebrations in New York City" were typical headlines.

But history has shown that there was no real peace in Europe.

9

As the second World War drew to a close, a new war was already beginning—mysterious, shadowy, elusive, and different from any other war. This new conflict—the cold war—would encompass the entire globe, divide the world, and change the life of every person on the planet Earth. And it would last for decades.

Dramatic and truly earth-shaking events were going on behind the scenes—events that were little noticed at the time by most Americans, who only wanted to get the war and the slaughter over with quickly. Hidden behind a barrage of propaganda, the Soviets' grand design for a Communist empire in Europe was unfolding. Wherever the Red armies moved, the Russians quickly brought in trained cadres of Communist political leaders to take control of the conquered territories.

In battle-torn Berlin, on April 30, 1945 (the day Hitler died), the world as men knew it was being remade, the old balance of power between nations was being swept away. The world's newspapers headlined Hitler's death as soon as the event became known, but another, vastly more important event, which also took place that same day in Berlin, went unreported. The Russians had labeled top secret the nonstop flight of a Soviet plane from Moscow to directly behind the battle lines in Berlin. A bold and daring Soviet scheme, carefully and secretly planned for two years, was soon to come out into the open. A new set of Communist leaders—Germans trained in Moscow's notorious Institute 99, which was a factory for political intrigue—arrived in Berlin with well-laid plans to partition the city. If the plans worked, they would be able to take over all of Berlin and eventually all of Germany.

Even a ruined Berlin was a great prize in the Cold War. Berlin was—and is—the most important city in Europe in the manufacture of machine tools, metals, and a thousand other things important in the balance of power between nations. A year later, in 1946, the Soviet Union's Foreign Minister, Vyacheslav M. Molotov, of the high, bulging forehead and icy dark eyes—a genius in international diplomacy—would sum up Berlin's importance: "What happens to Berlin, happens to Germany; what happens to Germany, happens to Europe." Berlin's strategic location as the crossroads of Europe, and its vast industrial output, make it a key to the control of Central Europe. A century and a half earlier Napoleon had written: "The road from Paris to Moscow leads through Berlin."

Soviet plans to take over Berlin were to have fateful consequences. The Red Army had already "liberated" Eastern Europe: Poland, Hungary, Rumania, Bulgaria, Latvia, Lithuania, and Estonia. Behind the Red armies, in violation of solemn Soviet pledges that the liberated countries would be free to choose their own postwar governments in secret elections, cadres of Communists had promptly been installed by the Kremlin to rule over these once independent countries. But Berlin and Germany represented a different kind of Soviet challenge to the West. Eastern Europe was held by the Red armies. Unless the Western allies, Britain and the United States in particular, were prepared to fight, there was nothing really effective they could do to free it from Soviet control. But Soviet aggression in Berlin and Germany would bring the Red armies into direct, face-to-face confrontation with the forces of the United States and Britain. The dangerous possibility of an armed conflict was great.

As the Russian airplane carrying the German Communist VIP's landed on the outskirts of Berlin, a steely-eyed man named Walter Ulbricht stepped out of the shadows of political intrigue in which he had lingered all his life and moved into the spotlight of world events. Immediately, Ulbricht and his party were whisked to the office of the Russian Commander where they took over political control of Berlin and East Germany.

Walter Ulbricht is a name to remember in connection with the Cold War. Shrewd, merciless, and quite willing to enslave his countrymen, Ulbricht's schemes have three times played a major role in bringing the world to the brink of nuclear war. As instigator of the Berlin blockade, of the Berlin crises of 1958 and 1961, and as the "architect" of the infamous Berlin Wall, Ulbricht became the symbol of the Cold War in Germany—the country destined to become the front-line battlefield between East and West.

Walter Ulbricht was little known to the world the day he and his party landed behind the thundering Russian howitzers. Years of Ulbricht's life had been spent in hiding. In 1928, Ulbricht had been elected from Leipzig to be a Communist member of

11

the German Reichstag, which was comparable to the American Congress. In 1933, when Hitler and the Nazis rose to power, Ulbricht fled Germany. For three years he led the secret, underground life of a Communist agitator in Paris and Prague. When the Spanish Civil War broke out, Ulbricht, under Stalin's personal orders, went to Spain. There he became a high Communist political commissar on the Loyalist side. He was noted for his merciless purges, which included the shooting of many of his close friends. After the Spanish Civil War ended, Ulbricht disappeared from public view. Then, in June, 1943, Ulbricht was seen in Moscow—the strong man behind the Free German Committee that Stalin was even then forming at Institute 99.

Of course, the aims of the Communists' Free German Committee were too important, too deeply disturbing, for news not to leak out to the Western allies. On February 4, 1945, at the Yalta Conference, held in Russia's Crimea, President Roosevelt and Prime Minister Churchill questioned Stalin sharply about Soviet plans in Germany. Stalin blandly denied any intent to use the Free German Committee and the Union of German Officers (German officer prisoners of war who had been captured by the Russians, brainwashed, and who had changed sides) to set up a Communist state in East Germany. *Pravda,* the official Soviet newspaper, was indignant that the Western countries had any such suspicions. The whole interpretation was "a tissue of lies . . . concocted by Fascist reactionaries," *Pravda* stated.

Nevertheless, on April 30, 1945, Walter Ulbricht's day had arrived. Backed by the Kremlin, Ulbricht was now the master of Berlin and all of East Germany.

Meanwhile, few Americans realized what was happening; they only knew that strange, puzzling things *were* happening. One fact that impressed itself on everybody's mind was the long, inexplicable delay that British, French, and American troops met in getting into Berlin. What should have been a routine military operation taking only a day or two, dragged on for weeks, and then months.

The major surrender conference held at Yalta, February 3–11, 1945, in many instances only reaffirmed decisions reached by the European Advisory Commission, which had met in Lon-

12

President Franklin D. Roosevelt (hat in hand) is greeted at the Yalta airport by Winston Churchill (middle) and Soviet Foreign Secretary Vyacheslav Molotov as a band plays the Russian national anthem.
—Wide World

don beginning in 1943. One of the major decisions of the Commission concerned the occupational zones and boundaries of Germany and the occupation of Berlin by troops of all the Allied powers. It was in these decisions, as it turned out, that the foundation for a split Berlin and a divided Germany was laid.

Although Western allied officers had flown to Berlin to sign the surrender documents on May 2, it was not until June 29 that an agreement was reached to permit Allied troops to enter Berlin. And this agreement hinged on a concurrent withdrawal of all occupational troops to their respective zones of occupation.

Thus for two critical months, from May 2 to July 4, all of Berlin was exclusively in Soviet hands. When Allied troops finally did march into the devastated Nazi capital, they found that every important civil official for every part of Berlin, including the American, British, and French zones, had been hand-picked by Ulbricht. Also, every important official was forced to live in the Soviet Zone, where the Russians could easily control him. In addition, the electric plant, the waterworks, the sanitation department—every necessary public service—were also located in the Soviet Zone.

Berlin was a strange, cold, and desolate place when General Lucius D. Clay and his American troops entered it in early July of 1945. They found a divided city, a divided Germany, and a divided world.

Chapter Two

CHURCHILL, TRUMAN AND STALIN MEET AT POTSDAM

"A shadow has fallen on the scenes so lately lighted by the Allied victory."
—Winston S. Churchill

In the last days of August, 1945, people in the United States and Britain were eagerly watching Japan. Would the Japanese quit the war soon? Tokyo was reeling under the fire-bomb raids of America's big B-29's, which set miles of the city's wood and paper houses ablaze. There was one hopeful sign—in April, 1945, the "moderate" Kanaro Suzuki, who had once been the victim of an attempted assassination by militant young Japanese military officers, was appointed prime minister. Later, it would be learned that both Suzuki and Emperor Hirohito wanted to surrender rather than continue the useless waste of lives. In a single raid on Tokyo, 175,000 dead and wounded were left behind in the flames!

It was plain that Japan was finished. The noose around the home islands was growing tighter each day. But Japan's fanatical military leaders refused to quit. When the Americans invaded, they would be defeated at the beaches, "Fight on!" the militarists commanded their people.

The prospect of invading Japan was grim. Estimates of the American dead and wounded ranged from 100,000 to a million. Nobody really knew how determined the resistance might be. On June 18, President Truman approved the top-secret Project Olympic—invasion plans for the Japanese home islands.

So, for most Americans, the Potsdam Conference, held July 17–August 2, 1945, was just a well-publicized sideshow. By this time, everybody knew that the Russians were being difficult, but wasn't President Truman going over to Germany to get everything straightened out?

President Truman and Secretary of State James Byrnes headed the large American delegation that arrived in Europe on the cruiser *Augusta*. Prime Minister Winston Churchill and Foreign Minister Anthony Eden of Britain and Premier Josef Stalin and Foreign Minister V. M. Molotov of the Soviet Union completed the list of main negotiators. Hundreds of military experts, diplomats, economists, and others accompanied them to the 10th-century city, Potsdam, on the outskirts of shattered Berlin.

Already the battle lines of the Cold War were drawn. Winston Churchill later wrote: "The world was in confusion. The main bond of common danger which had united the Great Allies had vanished overnight. The Soviet menace, to my eyes, had already replaced the Nazi foe. . . . I could not rid my mind of the fear that the victorious armies of democracy would soon disperse and that the real and hardest test still lay before us."

The outlines of the Soviet Union's plan to take over Poland, Eastern Europe, and as much of defeated Germany as possible were clear. At Yalta, the Soviet Union had promised that the former Axis allies—Hungary, Rumania, Bulgaria, Austria, and others—would be permitted to choose their own governments in free and secret elections. But where the Red Army conquered, Soviet puppets were installed and the Communists took over. What had happened in Rumania was typical. More than 14 months earlier, on April 2, 1944, when the Red Army had fought its way to the Rumanian border, the canny Molotov had issued a propaganda statement aimed at the West. Russia, the shrewd Foreign Minister said, wanted neither territory nor to change Rumania's social structure. But a Communist puppet government (the Ulbricht regime in East Germany would soon develop along these lines), promptly took over.

The looming Communist triumph in Poland was a bitter shock to the British. In 1939, Britain and France had gone to war to defend Polish soil against the Nazis. Now, at Potsdam, Churchill found himself stalemated by an adamant Stalin—with Poland firmly in Communist hands. Despite pledges given at the Teheran and Yalta conferences, of a democratic government in

Winston Churchill, Harry Truman and Josef Stalin at the Potsdam Conference.—U.S. Department of State

Poland, freely elected by the people in secret ballot, the Communists had installed Boleslaw Beirut as president.

The Potsdam Conference brought together the "Big Three": Winston Churchill, Britain's great wartime leader; Premier Josef Stalin of the Soviet Union; and Harry Truman, the new President of the United States (who was meeting the others for the first time).

What contrasts Churchill, Stalin, and Truman presented! It would have been hard to find three men of more differing backgrounds in the ways in which they reached the leadership of their nations. All were to be towering figures in the Cold War. Each of their stories is fascinating and important, too, as a guide to understanding their actions and decisions:

Harry Truman, America's new President, was a brisk, small man, as unpretentious as an old shoe. President Truman's rise in politics had astonished even himself, as he often stated. Born in Lamar, Missouri, on May 8, 1884, Truman had been a farm boy, milking cows and doing other chores. Then he went to Kansas City to work as a bank clerk. In World War I, Harry Truman first showed his promise as a leader when he rose to the rank of Captain of Artillery in the American Expeditionary Force. After getting out of the Army, Truman went into business for himself, setting up a clothing store. But, in the brief depression of 1921, his store failed. Then Harry Truman went into politics, becoming a judge in Kansas City. There was a notorious political machine in Kansas City at the time, but because Truman was widely known to be personally honest, the machine put him up as a candidate for United States senator. He won, and, to everybody's surprise, the humble man from Missouri became one of the nation's best senators, making a national reputation as chairman of a Senate committee to investigate government buying of arms and materials for the war. The Truman Committee did such an able job, saving the country billions of dollars, that in 1944, when the Democratic National Convention rebelled at renominating Vice-President Henry A. Wallace, Harry Truman was nominated the vice-presidential candidate in his place. Largely because of the unequalled popularity of Franklin D. Roosevlet, the Democratic ticket won the election in a landslide. As vice-president, Harry Truman was not a leading figure in the American Government. He was seldom consulted on the earth-shaking issues of winning the war and the peace. Then Franklin D. Roosevelt's sudden death catapulted Harry Truman into the eye of the gathering hurricane of world problems.

Winston Churchill: "Of course, Madam. *All* babies look like me!" This wry remark was made by the Prime Minister of Britain to a fond mother who had told Churchill that her new baby looked exactly like him. She actually came quite close to describing Churchill—in repose! He was cherubic and pink-faced, with just a sprinkle of fuzz for hair. A whole generation of people had noted Churchill's resemblance to babies. When upset or determined, however, Churchill's expressive face, with its jutting, out-thrust jaw, mirrored the famous British "bulldog" determination.

Whereas Harry Truman had been born poor, of a humble farm family, Winston Leonard Spencer Churchill was born of rich, aristocratic, and famous parents at Blenheim Palace, England, on November 30, 1874. His mother was Jenny Jerome, an American and a reigning international beauty of her day. His father was Lord Randolph Churchill. Interestingly, Winston Churchill, though later to be known as a scholar and brilliant writer of history who included among a myriad of assorted talents statecraft, oratory, painting, and bricklaying (to mention only a few), was a poor student in school. Young Winston did badly at St. George's School in Ascot and at Harrow, and barely scraped through in his studies at Sandhurst, the British military academy. Latin and Greek were difficult for him, but he excelled at English. The English sentence, he said later, is "a noble thing."

After graduation, Churchill's true-life adventures were more blood-and-thunder than some fiction. He served with a mounted regiment in India, grew bored when the fighting stopped, took leave, and covered the Boer War between Britain and South Africa as a war correspondent for a London newspaper. Churchill was captured by the Boers, and his dramatic stories of his escape made him a national hero when he returned to Britain. A long career in politics, with many ups and downs, followed. During World War I, Churchill was First Lord of the Admiralty. His work was brilliant, but he retired in disgrace when the British attempt to force through the Dardanelles failed. Out of office,

Churchill wrote books what were to become famous, took up painting as a hobby, and began warning people about the rising menace of the Nazi Party in Germany—at a time when few people considered Hitler very important. As Hitler grew in power and influence, Churchill, once more in Parliament, continued to issue warnings. In Britain's darkest hour, he became Prime Minister and symbolized British courage in the desperate struggle for Britain's life.

By the time of the Potsdam Conference, Winston Churchill was thoroughly alarmed. He had urged over and over again that differences with the Russians be ironed out *before* the Western armies left the territory they had conquered in Germany and retired to occupation zones agreed upon long before. The Americans, preoccupied by the continuing war with Japan, refused to hurry the conference. Later, Churchill made this observation:

> On July 1 the United States and British Armies began their withdrawal to their allotted zones, followed by masses of refugees. Soviet Russia was established in the heart of Europe. This was a fateful milestone for mankind.

Nor was that all. The Soviet Union menaced Turkey, demanding revision of the 1925 Soviet-Turkish pact. The revisions would give Russia special and exclusive privileges in the Black Sea, through the Dardanelles and the Bosphorus to the Mediterranean. In addition, Communist guerrillas were fighting a civil war in Greece aimed at taking over that nation. Also, the Soviet Union, which had occupied part of oil-rich Iran during the war against Germany, refused to evacuate its troops now that the Nazis were beaten. Everywhere, the Red Army was triumphant and on the march.

At Potsdam, Winston Churchill seemed at the height of his power. His leadership had pulled Britain from the edge of defeat to victory in history's most costly war. Supremely confident, Churchill had scheduled a British election, the ballots of which were already cast and in sealed boxes. (The ballots were not counted until three weeks after the election.) The Deputy Prime Minister of Britain, Clement Attlee, a mild, mousy little man who Churchill, with mingled contempt and affection called "a sheep in sheep's clothing," was tagging along with the British delegation to Potsdam. Nobody expected that Attlee would play an important role at Potsdam. Surely Churchill would be triumphantly re-elected leader of the British people!

Josef Stalin, Premier and absolute ruler of Russia, was the enigmatic and mysterious third member of the "Big Three." Photos show Stalin with thick eyebrows, dark eyes, brush-cut dark hair streaked with silver gray, and usually with a bluff, jovial smile. Soviet propagandists worked hard to paint an image of Stalin as hearty "Uncle Joe." But even in wartime, when the Russians were allies, the image just didn't come off. People remembered that Stalin had made a pact with Hitler in 1939 that had freed Hitler's hands to begin the second World War; that Stalin had participated with Hitler in the dismemberment of Poland and had ordered the ruthless murder of millions of kulaks —small Russian farmers who resisted having their land taken away from them to make huge collective farms.

Stalin was not the Soviet leader's real name, but one he took for political purposes. In Russian, it meant "Man of Steel," and "Man of Steel" well described Stalin. He had lived through purges, attempts to kill him, intrigues, and exile by the Czar of Russia's secret police.

Stalin was born Josef Dzhugashvili, and he was educated to be a priest! He was born December 21, 1879, in Gori, in the part of Russia called Georgia. His father was a poor shoemaker who died when Stalin was eleven. But the boy was bright, and got a scholarship to a theological seminary in Tiflis. At the seminary, Stalin proved more interested in politics than religion. He joined a secret organization of students studying the Communist doctrines of Karl Marx, and he was expelled. At once, he went underground—living and working in secret—and moved from place to place as he worked to overthrow the Czar's government. The Czar's secret police caught him and deported him to the icy wastes of Siberia, but not before Stalin had become important in the Bolshevik Party. Among the other tasks Stalin did for the Bolsheviks was the translation of the writings of Nikolai Lenin from Russian to Georgian. Stalin escaped from Siberia. He was caught again and returned to Siberia. Again he escaped.

In 1912, he first dropped the name Dzhugashvili and began to use the name Stalin. He was also appointed editor of *Pravda,* the Communist underground newspaper, in that year. Then came World War I. Russia fought against Germany and suffered massive defeats and enormous loss of life. The Czar was overthrown and replaced by a provisional government, which, in turn, fell before the onslaught of the Bolsheviks. Nikolai Lenin became head of state. Josef Stalin continued his rapid rise. In 1922, he was appointed Secretary General of the Communist Party. A series of intrigues, first against Lenin (whom rumor says he poisoned), then against Leon Trotsky, his main rival, and then a ruthless series of purges of lesser opponents gave Stalin iron control of the Soviet Government.

Stalin's enemies have called him one of the most ruthless and brutal men in history, and this is quite true. But he was much more than that. Stalin was also one of the most cunning and clever men in history. One of his speeches made in 1931 was prophetic: "We are one hundred years behind the advanced countries," Stalin bluntly said. "We must make good this lag in ten years. Either we do it, or they will crush us."

The prophecy of the "Man of Steel" proved uncannily correct. Exactly ten years later, the Nazi war machine of Adolf Hitler was unleashed upon the Soviet Union. American and British aid played a key role in saving the Soviet Union, but the factories and steel mills to which Stalin had given priority in Russia —often at the cost of famine for his people—enabled the Soviet Union to survive.

In a private telegram to President Truman, sent shortly before Potsdam, Winston Churchill uttered a fateful phrase: "An Iron Curtain is drawn down upon their front." Churchill urged a united British-American effort to save Eastern Europe.

Potsdam edges the southwest boundary of Berlin. At the beginning of the fateful conference, Berlin was still entirely in the hands of the Russians. But arrangements were being made for the British and the Americans to move into their previously agreed-upon occupation sectors. In exchange, U. S. and British forces would withdraw from huge areas of Central Germany to zones of occupation agreed upon in 1943. Both Churchill and Truman were taken on tours of Berlin. Both were deeply sobered by the ruin of the once beautiful city.

The Potsdam Conference quickly revealed that the Russians,

instead of working to smooth out the difficult problems that separated them from the West, were determined to hold onto all the territory the Red Army had taken, and to grasp for more. For example, on the problem of Poland's boundaries, the conference bogged down in frustrating disagreement. Earlier conferences had tentatively put Poland's western boundary at the eastern branch of the Neisse River. Now, the Red Army had put the Polish-German boundary at the western Neisse. This was because the Soviet Union had grabbed much of Poland's eastern territory and incorporated it into Soviet Russia. Poland's boundaries were to be moved far to the West. Many bitter words were exchanged about this and about the Soviet Union's breaking its other pledges in Eastern Europe. But Josef Stalin, behind his affable smile, really proved to be the "Man of Steel." He would budge not an inch on anything important. Aside from refusing to recognize Poland's western boundary, there was little Britain and the United States could do. The Red Army was in firm control. The Soviet troops probably could have been dislodged only by war, and that was out of the question. Having just finished the terrible war against the Nazis, with a seemingly long and bloody war with Japan still looming ahead, neither the British nor the Americans could have supported a conflict with the Soviet Union over Poland and Eastern Europe. So fas as Eastern Europe was concerned, the trump card—the Red Army's possession of the territory—was in Stalin's hands at Potsdam.

Some progress was made. An agreement was reached to try the Nazi war criminals for crimes against humanity. Final plans were laid for the exchange of territory in Allied control to the zones of occupation agreed upon earlier by the European Advisory Council representing Britain, the Soviet Union, and America. Later, this seemingly routine matter of occupational zones was to be of vital importance in the Berlin Blockade.

At Potsdam, Russian tactics roused the ire of the peppery Harry Truman. Twice the American President came close to stalking out of the conference. But the Soviets were thwarted in one of their biggest aims—to take gigantic reparations in industrial goods from the western zones of occupied Germany. Instead since starvation threatened the industrial western zones, Truman and Churchill insisted upon a barter—coal from the Rhur Valley in exchange for food from the agricultural Soviet-occupied zone.

In mid-conference, like a thunderclap, the results of the British election were announced. Churchill, Britain's great wartime leader, had been defeated by the Labour Party candidate, Clement Attlee! With Roosevelt dead and Churchill removed from the scene, Stalin alone of the original "Big Three" signed the Potsdam protocols in the ornate summer Palace of the Hohenzollerns, once the home of the royal family of Imperial Germany.

Potsdam was never intended to be a peace conference. The nagging disputes between East and West were supposed to be settled later. But the Cold War quickly became so bitter, so intense, that no peace conference was ever held. Potsdam resulted in frustration for both sides—as later events proved. For example, thirteen years afterward, on November 10, 1958 Nikita Khrushchev, then Soviet Premier, made a furious speech at a Polish Embassy reception in Moscow during which he denounced and attempted to declare null and void the decisions made at Potsdam.

On August 11, 1961, in a speech in Minneapolis, Minnesota, former President Harry S. Truman called the Russians "the biggest liars in the world," who had "broken every agreement made at Potsdam."

It is evident that neither side is very happy over Potsdam. In point of fact, it represented almost the final breakdown of harmony between the wartime allies who destroyed Hitlerism.

Two other things that happened at Potsdam were important: first, Britain and the United States joined together in an ultimatum to Japan to surrender. Second, at one of the lavish receptions, President Truman told Stalin that the United States had a "new bomb" that would shortly be used against Japan, which had refused the ultimatum to surrender.

"Good," Stalin said, seeming not much interested. Winston Churchill, who knew the best-kept secret of the war, was watching. He thought Stalin failed to really understand the importance of the American President's words. Later, it would be revealed that Stalin's efficient spy network had kept him informed of the awesome atomic secret, which would shortly change the world.

Chapter Three

A MUSHROOM-SHAPED CLOUD

"It is an awesome responsibility which has come to us."
—Harry S. Truman

Half a world away from Berlin, in strictest secrecy, events were taking place that would change the world, cast a mushroom-shaped shadow over the fate of mankind, and add an element of terror to the Cold War.

August 6, 1945, was an epochal day in world history. At 2:46 in the inky black morning darkness on the Pacific island of Tinian in the Marianas, a heavily loaded B-29 named the *Enola Gay* struggled into the air only a few feet from the end of the runway. The *Enola Gay* was part of the mysterious, shadowy 509th Bomb Group that had puzzled the other American flying teams on Tinian. The 509th never participated in any of the massive bombing raids over Tokyo or other Japanese cities. What was the 509th up to? Nobody knew, and crew members, who actually knew very little of their real mission, were sworn to the tightest secrecy.

The *Enola Gay,* under the command of Major Paul W. Tibbets, Jr., headed for Iwo Jima, 623 miles distant, in the company of three other B-29's of the 509th. One of the other planes was to take photographs, one was to take measurements on the special, 10,000-pound bomb the *Enola Gay* carried, and the third was to carry on if the *Enola Gay* should develop engine trouble and have to transfer its cargo at Iwo Jima. Meanwhile, a weather plane, *The Straight Flush,* had gone on ahead—to find the Japanese island of Shikoku covered with thick clouds—except for a break over the city of Hiroshima, the primary target of the *Enola Gay's* mission. *The Straight Flush,* in code tersely radioed back: "Bomb primary."

At ten minutes after eight o'clock, in brilliant sunshine, Hiroshima could be seen through the hole in the clouds. Crew members pulled on special goggles that would admit only light of one color—purple—and the bomb run began. The crew of the *Enola Gay* had spent many months practicing for this moment. At 31,000 feet, heading west, the bombardier, Major Tom Ferebee, searched intently for the aiming point, a bridge over the Ota River. A few seconds after 8:15 on that sunlit morning, the bomb-bay doors opened and the huge, 10,000-pound bomb, set by complex electronic mechanisms to explode about 1,850 feet above the ground, was released. Major Tibbets twisted the *Enola Gay* into a screaming, 160-degree turn to the right. Scientists had estimated that the plane would have to be at least eight miles distant—and going away—when the bomb exploded.

For 43 endless seconds, nothing happened.

Part of one building remains in the sea of rubble after an atomic bomb was dropped on Hiroshima in 1945. The building is now a museum and symbol of world peace.—United Press International

Then there was an eerie, silent, blinding flash of white light—
so powerful that it surpassed the sun. As soon as crew members
of the *Enola Gay,* blinking (some thought they had been
blinded by the intensity of the white light), could see again, the
center of the city of Hiroshima was missing. The explosion had
been a new type of bomb—an atomic bomb. It generated heat
up to 100,000,000 degrees. In some places, the heat was so intense that it melted blocks of granite.

Fantastic heat, shock waves, and thousands of raging fires
swept the stricken city. A mushroom-shaped cloud, four miles
high, formed. Then the *Enola Gay* headed back to Tinian. In
Hiroshima, there would be 70,000 casualties.

The next morning, *The New York Times,* in headlines much
like those all over the world, recorded the birth of the Atomic
Age:

FIRST ATOMIC BOMB DROPPED ON JAPAN;
MISSILE IS EQUAL TO 20,000 TONS OF TNT;
TRUMAN WARNS OF 'A RAIN OF RUIN'
New Age Ushered In
Hiroshima Is Target
"Impenetrable" Cloud Of
Dust Hides City After
Single Bomb Strike

There were other headlines in the days to come: "Soviets Declare War On Japan; Attack Manchuria, Tokyo Says" and
"Atom Bomb Loosed on Nagasaki," describing a second and
less lethal attack on the Japanese city of Nagasaki. Then, on
August 10: "Truman Warns Japan—Quit Or Be Destroyed."
On August 14: "Japan Surrenders Unconditionally." World War
II was history. *Stars And Stripes,* the Army newspaper, headlined the single word PEACE on its front page. But *was* there
peace? With the force of atomic energy unlocked, man would
soon have the means of destroying the planet on which he lived.

Should the atomic bomb have been dropped on Hiroshima
and Nagasaki? In later years, there would be a world-wide debate on the morality of using such a destructive weapon. President Truman stoutly defended his authorization of the use of the
A-bomb as necessary to win the war. Winston Churchill, in *The*

Second World War, said there was never "a moment's discussion" as to whether the bomb should be used or not. "To avert a vast, indefinite butchery, to bring peace to the world, to lay healing hands upon its tortured peoples by a manifestation of overwhelming power . . . seemed, after all our toils and perils, a miracle of deliverance."

Almost at once, another question began to trouble people. Could the atomic bomb be controlled? And what about the Russians? Would they be given the secret of the A-bomb?

President Harry Truman made it crystal clear that they would not. In a statement, President Truman posed the troublesome dilemma of controlling nuclear weapons that haunts the world to this day:

> The atomic bomb is too dangerous to be loose in a lawless world. That is why Great Britain, Canada and the United States, who have the secret of its production, do not intend to reveal that secret until means have been found to protect ourselves and the rest of the world from the danger of total destruction . . . we must constitute ourselves trustees of this new force—to prevent its misuse and to turn it into channels of service to mankind . . . it is an awesome responsibility which has come to us. . . .

Chapter Four

THE COLD WAR ENGULFS THE BALKANS AND THE MIDDLE EAST

"The lines were first clearly drawn here."
—Mohammed Reza Pahlavi, Shah-in-Shah of Iran

A war-wearied world was disturbed to read in newspaper reports of January 10, 1946, that "immigrants and strangers attacked voters" near an obscure village in far-away Iran.

News accounts, reported by the Associated Press, gave the details. "Five killed in Iranian factional clashes," read one newspaper story, "in fighting between partisans in Russian-occupied northern Iran."

The disorders were reported as occurring near Zenjan, 200 miles northeast of the capital city of Teheran, and at Kazvin, 90 miles north of Teheran. The reports said that "Democratic insurgents" were involved in Zenjan and at Kazvin, the gateway to the Russian-held Azerbaijan.

Most people's minds were on other things that day. American audiences were introduced to the first Kaiser automobile, the newest entry on the postwar scene. In New York City, a strike of telephone company employees occupied the biggest slice of news space.

The same day, New Yorkers watched a giant victory parade along Fifth Avenue, in honor of the foot soldiers of World War II who had returned under the banner of the popular Major General James M. Gavin. The avenue and crosstown 42nd Street were draped in flags and bunting to welcome the returning heroes.

Fears were lulled by the fact that the "Big Four" foreign ministers were again attempting to solve the problems of the long-delayed Italian peace treaty draft in London. Its tangled provisions, however, were snarled by details concerning other nations—especially Rumania and Bulgaria.

The London Conference reported that Rumania would be recognized despite Western allied misgivings over the Soviet Union's assurances of free elections and "other freedoms"—assurances often voiced by the Communist-controlled governments but still not forthcoming. The Bulgarian question was another serious matter for dispute. All of the allies had agreed in Moscow that the Russians would arrange for the enlargement of the Bulgarian Fatherland Front Government, with members from opposition parties being included. This, the Western allies learned, was not taking place.

The West had, in fact, already lost in Rumania. In September, 1945, King Michael had appealed to the Allies to set up a representative government to replace the Communist-dominated cabinet of Peter Groza. Britain and America could do nothing but protest. Groza, visiting Moscow, received the red-carpet treatment. "I am happy that I tread the Moscow earth. . . . Light comes from the East," the Rumanian Communist leader declared.

In Bulgaria, the Communist-dominated Fatherland Front had established itself firmly. No enlargement to include representative opposition party members would ever take place.

A wave of shock and pessimism replaced the lighthearted optimism of the close of the war. Free people everywhere began to realize what the informed already knew: that East and West were deeply split.

Then on the ninth day of the first session of the General Assembly meeting of the United Nations, the Iranian situation again dominated the news. Iranian representatives to the United Nations formally requested the Security Council to "look into her disputes with the Russians" and charged the Soviet Union with "interference in Iran's internal affairs."

At the same time both Syria and Lebanon asked that both Britain and the United States withdraw their troops. Thus, early in the shaky peace following the greatest war mankind had ever known, three members of the Security Council were charged with improper use of their troops in the Middle East. And affairs in the Balkans looked bleak indeed.

In Greece, the Cold War had long since turned into a hot war. For more than a year, bloody clashes had taken place between the Communist-dominated E. A. M. and E. L. A. S. forces and pro-Western forces.

The roots of the Greek civil war went far back. In December, 1944, when the Nazis evacuated Greece, the Communist guerrillas tried to take over Athens and the Greek Government by force. Winston Churchill had created an international furor when he refused to permit it.

To Lieutenant General Sir R. M. Scobie, commandant of the 5,000 British troops who had landed and fought the Nazi troops outside Athens, Churchill had wired: "We have to hold and dominate Athens. It would be a great thing for you to succeed without bloodshed if possible, but also with bloodshed if necessary."

Events proved that bloodshed was necessary to keep Greece free.

On December 10, 1944, tremendous pitched battles, involving tanks and artillery, were fought between the British Army and the Greek Communists. In one day, there were an estimated 8,000 casualties.

Churchill explained his incredible act: To save Greece from Communism, even at the risk of disrupting the war-time alliance:

> I directed General Scobie to assume complete control of Athens. If I am blamed for this action, I will gladly accept dismissal by the House of Commons. But if I am not dismissed, make no mistake, we shall persist in this policy of clearing Athens and the Athens region of all rebels to the constitutional government of Greece.

Churchill raised a tremendously important question before the gravely disturbed House of Commons.

Who are the friends of democracy and how is the word "democracy" to be interpreted?

The last thing that resembles democracy is mob law with

bands of gangsters with deadly weapons forcing their way into Greek cities, seizing police stations and key points of the government, and endeavoring to introduce a totalitarian regime . . . Do not let us rate democracy so low. . . Democracy is not based upon terrorism, but on reason, on fair play . . .

Athens had been saved, but at the time Iran dramatically brought its case against Soviet Russia to the United Nations, the Communist threat was still strong.

Iran's case before the United Nations reminded the world that Russian, British, and American troops had entered Iran in 1941 to open a secure route for Allied supplies going to Russia. An agreement had been reached guaranteeing that Iranian sovereignty would be respected and that all troops would be withdrawn 6 months after the war had ended. Britain had suggested at the London Conference of Foreign Ministers that, "since the war was over," troops leave Iran in mid-December, 1945. The Americans had left by January, 1946. But the Soviet troops had only partially withdrawn by the deadline.

Now came ominous word of Russian interference in Iranian governmental affairs in the Azerbaijan. It was not the first time this had happened. Living border-to-border with the giant, sprawling Soviet state, Iran (formerly Persia) had always followed a cautious path with her mighty neighbor to the north. When the Russian Revolution came, in 1917, Iran was one of the first countries to give diplomatic recognition to the Lenin government. Lenin himself then declared that all small nations should be fully independent, and the 1921 Irano-Soviet Treaty of Friendship was drawn up.

"But the hope was doomed to disappointment," declared Shah Mohammed Reza Shah Pahlavi in his autobiography. During the negotiations of that treaty, the Soviets "committed an astounding act of aggression; they landed troops at Iran's Caspian port of Enzeli [later renamed Pahlavi] to support Kuchik Khan, the rebel Iranian leader." The Shah reported that this support enabled Kuchik Khan to establish, "with amazing impudence," what was called the Soviet Republic of Gilan.

Later in December, 1945, the Russians boldly sponsored two

puppet governments within Iranian borders. One was called "The Kurdish Republic of Mahabad"; the other, the "Autonomous Government of Azerbaijan." When the deadline, March 3, 1946, came for the promised withdrawal of foreign troops from Iranian soil, the Russians remained.

The Russians massed tanks with auxiliary units and supporting infantry in Iran. The United States and Britain strongly urged the Soviets to comply with their agreements, to no avail. On March 21, Iran seconded its original complaint to the Security Council. Iran's Ambassador Ala presented the Shah's demands again in what the Shah later called "one of the most brilliant and dramatic presentations in the annals of the Council."

Five days later the Soviet Delegate to the United Nations, Andrei Gromyko, announced that all Soviet forces would be out of Iran "in five or six weeks." By May 9, the troops were gone. Iran, though still faced with tumultuous years and great struggle ahead, continued independent.

Nobody doubted that America's possession of the atomic bomb, which stood behind the stern American warnings to the Soviet Union to leave Iran, was more persuasive than arguments in the United Nations.

The Iranian incident made familiar a new face in the great drama of the Cold War, that of the Shah-in-Shah, Mohammed Reza Pahlavi. It is the most youthful face in the entire Cold War drama. At 22 the sole heir to the Iranian crown was named Emperor of Iran following the abdication of his father Reza Shah in 1942. Reza Shah had himself wrested the government from the failing feudal hands of Ahmed Shah, the last of the Qajar rulers, in 1923. At the Teheran Conference in the winter of 1943, Churchill labeled the young Shah "gifted."

"Courageous" might have also been aptly applied to the youthful monarch. When the war had ended and the 6-month period of time in which Russian, British, and American troops were to have withdrawn from Iranian soil elapsed, the young Shah sent Iranian troops to help oust the Russians from Azerbaijan. In his protest to the United Nations the young Shah had to bypass his own Prime Minister, Qavam, to see to it that Iran's forceful protest was registered before the Security Council. The Prime Minister was frightened of the mighty Red Army. The

Shah played a successful game in forcing the Russians to leave the country by luring them with the hopes of possible oil concessions if they would leave Iranian soil. When postwar elections were ordered for all Iran, including the "autonomous" Azerbaijan province, the Russians found themselves in the embarrassing position of having to stand back and see their puppet regime toppled. Iranian troops entered the area in December, 1946. Later their pro-Russian Kurdish puppet regime also collapsed.

Russian troops leave Meshed, Iran, in March, 1946.—Wide World

"I think historians of the future will say that the Cold War really began in Iran," reports the Shah in his book *Mission For My Country*. "The lines were first clearly drawn here."

The Azerbaijan affair had fateful consequences for all Americans. America for the first time began to play a major role in the Middle East.

Iran was a Western victory, but efforts to win Yugoslavia to the side of the West during the first postwar year, 1946, failed. Since 1929 Yugoslavia had been a generally unharmonious union of South Slavic peoples, including Serbs, Croats, Slovenes, and Montenegrins. The *new* Yugoslavia included not only the Balkan states of Montenegro and Serbia but peoples of Bosnia, Croatia, Dalmatia, Slovenia, Herzegovina and Macedonia. It had suffered frightfully during the Nazi occupation of the country from 1941 to 1945. In the three-day Nazi bombing of Belgrade tens of thousands died in the holocaust. Later, massive retaliatory measures were carried out against the invading Germans. Heroic Yugoslavs (the name means "South Slavs") took to the hills and formed resistance groups that effectively continued the fight against the Nazi invaders. The most important resistance members were the Cetniks (or Chetniks), the followers of General Draza Mihajlovic, and the Partisans under Tito, as he styled himself.

In the power struggle between these two, Tito emerged victorious and another notable face entered the Cold War drama.

Originally Josip Broz, the son of a Croatian blacksmith, Tito rose to become the pre-eminent leader of the Yugoslavs and a world leader who one day would be the first to crack the monolithic Communist control of the so-called East European satellite nations. Tito had fought with the Austro-Hungarian Army in the First World War and had been captured in Russian. In the Russian civil war, 1918–1920, he volunteered for service in the Red Army. Later, returning to his Croatian homeland as a metalworker, Tito became an active union organizer and reportedly a Communist agent and political agitator. He served a prison term for some years in his native Croatia for these political activities.

Tito's army of Partisans, an estimated 200,000 strong, played a heroic role against the Nazis. Tito was supported from the first by Soviet Russia, though many of his followers were not Communist. Later England and the United States also gave him aid for his guerrilla resistance movement. In May, 1943, the British established contact with Tito's forces and sent a small armed force to his aid by dramatic parachute drops into the Partisan mountain stronghold of Bosnia. The phenomenal growth of Tito's military strength and his obvious popular support led the Allies to back his provisional government in late 1944. Later, the British Ambassador to the Royal Yugoslav Government of King Peter, in exile in Cairo, would advise his government in London: "Our policy must be based on three new factors: The Partisans will be the rulers of Yugoslavia. They are of such value to us militarily that we must back them to the full, subordinating political considerations to military. It is extremely doubtful whether we can any longer regard the monarchy as a unifying element in Yugoslavia."

In elections held in Yugoslavia in November, 1945, Tito's Communist-dominated National Liberation Front swept into office. (The Royalists, in protest, abstained from voting.) King Peter was deposed.

The Soviet Union was elated. It appeared that Premier Tito's Federal People's Republic of Yugoslavia was just another in the series of puppet regimes the Soviet Union had established and that Tito would doubtless docilly take orders from the Kremlin. But in less than two years Josef Stalin was to receive a stunning surprise.

Chapter Five

BERLIN AGAIN

> *"What happens to Berlin, happens to Germany; what happens to Germany, happens to Europe."*
> —Soviet Foreign Minister, V. M. Molotov, 1946

Hunger, famine, defeat, and despair stalked the rubble-strewn streets of ruined Berlin during the terrible winter of 1945–46. The trees in the parks were chopped down for firewood; there was no coal or fuel available for heating homes. All of Europe shivered and most people went to bed hungry. With memories of Nazi concentration camps and the ruin and death the Germans had inflicted on their neighbors still fresh, they got scant sympathy—though they suffered most of all.

General Lucius Clay, the American commander in Berlin, recalls in his book, *Decision In Germany*, that it was far from rare to see people in the streets faint from hunger. The official food ration was 1,500 calories—far less than the minimum amount of food needed to sustain health. Actually, few Berliners got that much to eat. There simply was not enough food and fuel for all of Europe. The Germans, who were blamed for the universal misery, were the last to get relief supplies.

In July, when American and British troops entered the one-time Nazi capital, they were welcomed wildly and frantically by the Berliners as liberators. The people were terrified of the Soviets, who had taken partial revenge for the atrocities inflicted on the Russian people. "The smell of death" was in the air, one correspondent wrote, commenting on the stench of unburied corpses in the mountains of rubble.

Factories and businesses in the Western sectors had been stripped clean of machinery, food, and everything of value. When the Western powers protested that it was a violation of the Potsdam agreement to leave a starving and destitute people to be fed, the Russians shrugged, blandly saying that this was "reparation in kind." The factory machinery and other things were to go to the Soviet Union in payment for the destruction wrought by the Nazis. But the railroad system between East Germany and the Soviet Union broke down, and millions of dollars worth of badly-needed equipment sat on railroad flatcars, rusting in rain and sleet until it was worthless to anyone.

The summer of 1945 had seen dangerous clashes between Russian and Western troops. Unter den Linden, once Berlin's most glittering street, lay in ruins. Huge posters of Josef Stalin lined the bomb-cratered boulevard. The Hohenzollern Palace and the Altes Museum were tangled ruins. The Soviets had issued an order "freezing" all the people who lived in their sector. Nobody could move into the British or American sectors under penalty of arrest and imprisonment. (But hordes of people secretly fled into West Berlin anyway.) All of the officials of Berlin had been forced to move into the eastern, Russian Sector —where the Soviets could control them. In the Soviet Zone of Germany farms were broken up and taken over by Walter Ulbricht's government. The decrees of the Communist regime confiscated almost everything worth owning.

Most amazing of all, the Soviets arrogantly refused at first to yield their offices to the Western allied officers in the British and American sectors. "Things are not ready," was the Soviet excuse.

American tempers seethed. "The Russians are running all of Berlin," Colonel Frank Howley muttered to newspaper reporters. Finally, the Western allies had enough. Under cover of darkness, they moved the Russian office equipment out of Western sector headquarter buildings, then took over their own offices.

The existence of the desperate food shortage was underlined by the streams of Germans still fleeing the Russian Zone, East Germany, and Poland and other nations taken over by the Soviets. More than 14 million men, women and children poured into the British, French, and American occupation zones of Germany. They came with only the few items of clothing and possessions that they could carry.

On October 1, 1945, General of the Armies Dwight David Eisenhower (later to be president of the United States), released some disturbing facts in a report on the American occupation of Germany: There would be no coal produced for heating homes during the bitter-cold winter, less than one tenth of Germany's bombed-out factories could be operated, only one worker in ten had a job, and business was at a standstill. Prices had skyrocketed. As a result of General Eisenhower's report, the United States began a stepped up program of sending food to its recently defeated enemy.

Meanwhile, in tense Berlin, Russian and Western troops, armed and edgy, stood face-to-face as the Cold War grew more chilly every day.

New Year's Day, 1946, was typical of the growing friction between United States and British troops on the one side and Soviet troops on the other. Corporal Mello Ciccone of Philadelphia was shot and killed and the German girl with him seriously wounded by a trigger-happy Russian soldier. Corporal Ciccone was the third American soldier shot to death in a single week by Soviet soldiers.

The Kommandatura, made up of the American, British, French, and Soviet commandants, was supposed to govern Berlin. But from the first, the Russian *nyet* brought to a halt any real attempt to solve Berlin's problems. General Clay wrote angrily of the Russian sabotage. The Soviet veto resulted in "trifles" being taken up, General Clay said, but the vital problems of food, housing, reconstruction, and employment were sabotaged.

A typical Kommandatura ruling was that bicycling, weight lifting, and mountain climbing would be forbidden sports for Germans, while football, volleyball, basketball, and baseball were all right. The former resembled too closely the Hitler Youth sports and were verboten, the Russians insisted.

Meanwhile many helpless Berliners were literally freezing and starving to death in bitterly cold, windowless, bombed-out hovels.

The Soviet strategy in Germany, until the dramatic elections of October, 1946, was to create chaos by blocking the Kommandatura, and to wait out the American departure from

Europe. In the friendly days of wartime cooperation, Franklin D. Roosevelt had once remarked to Churchill and Stalin at Teheran that they had better not count on America's presence in Europe for longer than two years. The Soviets also remembered the rapid pull-back of the United States from Europe after World War I. Other events encouraged the Soviets to hope that the United States would soon leave. In January, 1946, a series of giant "Bring Them Home" drives broke out all over the United States. Impatient wives, mothers, and fathers of American servicemen stationed abroad, weary of war and disillusioned by the rapid souring of the peace, staged parades and demonstrations demanding that American soldiers be brought home. The war was over, wasn't it? Then why was the government keeping their husbands, brothers, and sweethearts overseas? "Bring them home," the demonstrators demanded.

On January 13, 1946, the "Bring Them Home" movement spread to Berlin. Demonstrations were staged by war-weary and bored occupation troops. General Joseph T. McNarney requested the soldiers to stop the demonstrations, and harried senior officers in Berlin expressed themselves as being "gravely concerned." They were more than that. The demonstrations bordered on outright mutiny. In the United States, General Dwight D. Eisenhower issued a statement deploring the "Bring Them Home" drives as blinding the United States to the responsibilities of the German occupation. Other officials said that United States prestige was being lowered. Spokesmen for the Soviet Union made no comment, but news reports described them as discreetly gleeful. At home, people were bewildered and reluctant to face the reality of The Cold War. Senator Arthur Vandenberg of Michigan, the leading Republican spokesman on the Senate Foreign Relations Committee, voiced the bewilderment of the public when he asked: "What is Russia up to? We ask it in Eastern Europe and the Dardanelles, in Italy, in Iran, in Tripolitania, in the Baltic and the Balkans, in Poland."

And then on March 5, 1946, came the dramatic moment which crystallized the thinking of the United States and the free world. Westminster College in tiny Fulton, Missouri, became the scene of world attention for a day, and it is even now associated with a phrase that will live in history. President Truman invited Winston Churchill, then a member of the British Parliament and no longer Prime Minister, to visit the United States. Everywhere Churchill went, he received a hero's welcome. And what better place to give the main speech of his visit than in President Truman's home state of Missouri? There was plenty of good-natured fun on the trip to Fulton. Mr. Churchill joined President Truman at the controls in the locomotive of the *Presidential Special* as it sped through Maryland and West Virginia countryside amid the first green of coming spring.

But the jocular mood had vanished when Winston Churchill spoke at Fulton after receiving an honorary degree. Even as the academic procession was forming, Yugoslav troops under the new Communist regime were surrounding the city of Trieste, uttering bellicose threats to take it by force.

"An Iron Curtain," Churchill gravely said, had descended across Europe. An "Iron Curtain dividing Europe is not what we fought for," said the former Prime Minister. Churchill proposed a United States-British association to curb what he described as "the expansion and proselytizing tendencies" of the Soviets. Churchill predicted a new "dark era in Europe":

> The English speaking peoples must maintain an overwhelming preponderance of power on their side until the highroads of the future will be clear, not only for us but for all, not only for our time, but for a century to come.

In describing the occupation by Russian troops of much of Eastern Europe and of the political pressures being applied by Moscow, he said, "this is certainly not the liberated Europe we fought to build up. Nor is it one which contains the essentials of permanent peace."

The speech shocked many Americans into thoughtful reappraisal of what action must be taken. Many others, however, continued to be complacent. "Selective service is going out May 15" replied Senator Edwin Johnson of Colorado to Selective Service Director General Lewis Hershey's plea for an extension of the draft.

Meanwhile, on the day Churchill spoke, a sensational revelation of the secret, underground war of spies, informers, and saboteurs came to light. Colonel Frank Howley, who was in charge of the Berlin branch of the United States Office of Military Government, announced the cracking of a spy ring inside the American Military Government, aimed at taking over the vital Schöneberg section of Berlin. Twelve Germans, working for the Americans, Howley charged, were secretly Communists, and had conspired to hire key officials who were also secretly Communists. The charges averred that in the American Zone the twelve blocked the hiring of any person not secretly cleared by the local Communist secretary. The defendants were tried by a military court martial of United States Army officers, were convicted, and received five-year prison sentences.

The Russian response to Winston Churchill's "Iron Curtain" speech was not unexpected. Josef Stalin denounced Churchill as "a dangerous warmonger," and, on March 23, 1946, Stalin began what newspapers described as "a peace offensive." In an interview, Stalin declared that the Soviet Union "does not want war" and "will stake its hopes for peace on the United Nations Organization." Quite evidently, however, Soviet delegates to the United Nations did not get the message—or secretly got a quite different message—from Comrade Stalin. For only four days after Stalin's praise of the United Nations, the Soviet delegation staged its first walkout on the deliberations of the United Nations. The Soviet Union's veto in the Security Council kept Iran's charge that the Soviet Union was interfering in her internal affairs from being acted upon.

As 1946 wore on, the Cold War deepened and widened. The Chinese civil war, which had smoldered quietly during the Japanese occupation of China, erupted in renewed fury. On April 20, the free world, intent upon the crises in Germany, the Balkans, and the Middle East, was stunned by the victory of Mao Tse-tung's troops over those of Chiang Kai-shek, with the Chinese Communist capture of the vital city of Changchun. In Berlin, the last vestige of cooperation between East and West vanished when the Soviet Union's greatest war hero, General Georgi Zhukov, winner of a chestful of medals for his role in the defense of Stalingrad, the capture of Berlin, and other battles, was replaced. Field Marshal Zhukov's "crime" in the eyes of Stalin was having the appearance, at least, of being friendly to the Western powers. His replacement, General Vassily D. Sokolovsky, was icy and rock-hard. Meanwhile, in the British House of Commons, Winston Churchill warned that "the seeds of World War Three" were being sown in Russian-occupied Eastern Europe.

Two headline stories appeared on June 14th and 15th, 1946. On the 14th, the United States, well aware of the awesome power it held in the atomic bomb, sought some way in which the destructiveness of atomic weapons could be controlled. In the United Nations, an unprecedented plan was offered by Bernard Baruch, on behalf of the American Government. The United States proposed to share American atomic energy secrets and to surrender America's stockpile of atom bombs to a "world atomic department." The Soviet Union's Foreign Minister, Andrei Gromyko, rejected Baruch's proposal and suggested another that had no provisions for international inspection. In addition, the Russians wanted a veto over the atomic control commission which could paralyze all effective action in case the Soviet Union should break its word. With so many broken Soviet promises in Europe, Iran, and elsewhere serving as a grim warning, President Truman and his advisers were determined not to let the Soviet Union have the secret of the atom bomb without some safeguards that it would not be misused.

The following day, another sensation made the headlines—this time in Canada, seemingly far from the Cold War. Any complacency that the Kremlin did not have spies and secret agents everywhere was shattered. In a sensational spy trial, Fred Rose, a member of the Canadian Parliament, was convicted of being a spy for the Soviet Union. Rose, the Canadian indictment charged, had passed along top government secrets to the Russians.

Years later, historians might look back and understand more clearly why the Soviet Union refused to accept the secret of the atomic bomb, *if* it had any provision for inspection attached. Soviet spies were already well along in their secret work of stealing and sending to the Soviet Union the many pieces of the puzzle of how to make an atom bomb. In the United Nations, Gromyko continued to offer only a plan that excluded inspection on Soviet soil. It was totally unacceptable to the West.

Half a month later, the mighty atom gave mankind a new and even more awe-inspiring demonstration of its power. The United States and Britain conducted A-bomb tests on remote Bikini Atoll in the Pacific. An atom bomb dropped from a height of five miles above the shimmering blue waters on which floated a target fleet of seventy-three ships (left over from the Second World War) sank five vessels outright and damaged fifty-one others. The damage done by radioactivity was even more frightening than the fiery mushroom cloud and the blast. Ninety percent of the animals confined in pens on the target ships were damaged by radiation. Scientists announced that most of the animals suffered from a falling blood count. The news was ominous. If a nuclear war should ever break out many more millions of people might suffer death or injury from nuclear fallout than would be killed by the bombs.

The United States atomic bomb secret was an important plus for the free world. But still the Communists gained ground— at a frightening pace. In Yugoslavia, the Communist Government triumphed in the power struggle and sentenced the pro-Western General Draža Mihajlović and eight of his top leaders to death. The charge was collaboration with the Nazis. In China, the Communist civil war picked up steam. The Chinese Communists announced an all-out mobilization in the area they controlled. On August 20, relations between the United States and Yugoslavia reached a crisis. The Yugoslav Government shot down an unarmed American transport plane, killing five American airmen. Thoroughly aroused, President Truman sent a note to Tito, giving the Yugoslavs forty-eight hours in which to "give satisfaction" for the deaths. The downing of an American plane was more important than just a confrontation between the United States and little Yugoslavia. Behind the Yugoslavs stood the might of the Soviet Union's Red Army, which far outnumbered American forces in Europe. The ultimatum raised the possibility of a confrontation between the United States and the Soviet Union. Some international observers saw the Yugoslav downing of an American plane as a test of the United States' will to defend its rights with force, if need be.

If the shooting down of the unarmed American plane was a test instead of just an unhappy "accident," as the Yugoslavs

A mushroom-shaped cloud rises off Bikini Atoll following atomic bomb test.—U.S. Department of State

said, the United States emerged the unhappy victor of the tragic clash. Within the forty-eight-hour deadline, the Yugoslavs apologized and paid an indemnity to the families of the dead United States airmen.

For a month, no great crisis occurred on the international scene and the world breathed a little easier. Then, as it would so often in the years to come, a crisis began slowly to develop in divided Berlin. The Potsdam and other Allied agreements provided that Germany was not to be split up into airtight zones and the same agreement was made about Berlin. Each of the "Big Three" Allies—Russia, Britain, and the United States—was to have its sector of occupation. (The French Sector had been carved out of the United States and British sectors in an agreement among the Allied wartime partners.) Freedom of movement was agreed upon, and Germany and Berlin were to be governed as a whole.

Earlier the Russians had drastically restricted freedom of the people to go from their zone or sector to another, but there was still a moderate amount of freedom.

Then, in September and October of 1946, with Berlin still in ruins, with barely more than the rubble cleared, with hunger and unemployment still everywhere, a strange thing happened. The East Berlin Communists and the British, French, and Americans found themselves deeply involved in—of all things —wooing the defeated Germans in an election campaign! Nobody suspected it, but the election results were to be far more important than anybody dreamed, for the result would mark a sharp turning in Russia's strategy and actions in divided Germany.

The election was for city officials in Berlin—the first, (and, as it turned out, also the last) free election held since World War II in *all* sectors of the divided city.

As the campaign began, the Communists seemed to have every advantage. The Soviet Union held very strong cards. At a massive political rally, for instance, Otto Grotewohl, Walter Ulbricht's beefy, red-faced right-hand man, announced that the Soviet Union had graciously—through the efforts of the Communist SED party—agreed to release 125,000 captured German prisoners of war being held in the Soviet Union. Mothers, wives, and other family members, desperately anxious about missing sons and husbands whom they had not seen for years went limp with relief. The Communist SED party was not above trafficking in human misery to gain votes.

Another announcement by Otto Grotewohl told Berliners that increased rations would be available in the Soviet Sector and would be given to all Berliners who came to the Soviet Zone. Also, allotments of shoes were announced for 65,000 Berlin schoolchildren. It may be hard to realize now how important these shoes were. But reports by social service workers in 1946 declared that thousands of Berlin children could not attend school because they had no shoes. For hungry, malnourished people living amid ruins, the promise of more food was tempting bait to vote for Communist-backed candidates.

Then came the vote. As the ballots were counted, the Communists were stunned. The pro-Western Social Democratic Party received 49 percent of the ballots cast—nearly half! The pro-Western Christian Democratic Party's candidates got 22 percent. The Communist SED Party got only 19 percent—less than one vote in five!

Never again would the Soviet Union permit free elections in their sector. From 1946 onward, elections were held in East Berlin only on Communist terms—with a slate of hand-picked Communist candidates running unopposed.

Berlin's critical election results left the Communists stunned and furious. West German sources later charged that thousands of East German men were "kidnapped" from the streets of East Berlin and shipped to Siberia and Russia for slave labor in retaliation for the lopsided vote.

The Berlin election was important far beyond the borders of Germany. It intensified the Cold War. At Potsdam, in a moment of candor, Stalin had said of the nations that bordered the Soviet Union: "A freely-elected government in any of these countries would be anti-Soviet, and that we cannot allow."

The results of the Berlin election confirmed Stalin's fears. The Soviet Union had lost in the trial by free election. The next challenge would be by bullets, not ballots. And it would come soon.

Chapter Six

THE TRUMAN DOCTRINE
AND THE MARSHALL PLAN

*"The Towers Of The Kremlin Cast A
Long Shadow."*
—George F. Kennan

Having lost the free appeal to the voters in Berlin (a later Secretary of State, John Foster Dulles, declared that no country ever went *voluntarily* behind the Iron Curtain), the Communists turned from propaganda to force. Perhaps to counter the electoral disaster, the Soviet-backed guerrilla war in the mountains of Greece was stepped up, and Soviet pressure on Turkey to grant bases and other concessions along the strategic Dardanelles —backed by naked hints of force if the bases were not granted —was intensified.

A brilliant American diplomat, George F. Kennan, Counselor of the United States Embassy in Moscow, thought that these months were very important—that Americans were abandoning any last, lingering false hopes that the reconstruction of Europe after the war could be carried on by cooperation with the Russians. In memoranda to the State Department, Kennan pointed out that the Soviet Union had a vested interest in hoping that the rebuilding of Western Europe would fail—unless it was rebuilt under men subservient to the Kremlin. Kennan would later become famous as the "Mr. X", who wrote an article in *Foreign Affairs* magazine advocating an American policy of "containment" of the Soviet Union. Kennan's containment theory was to have vast impact. It became a catch phrase among diplomats. Broadly speaking, the United States would now attempt to "contain" the Soviet Union and the mighty Red Army to the sphere it now held.

March, 1947, was an historic month. Britain and France

signed a fifty-year treaty of peace and friendship—an action immediately denounced by the Soviet Union as being directed against it. Two days later, the American State Department launched an angry protest against the Soviet Union for interference in the domestic affairs of Hungary. Newspapers pointed out that the protest seemed mostly for the record. Red Army troops were stationed in Hungary in force. The United States and British forces were far away. A few weeks earlier, the Ameri-

In a joint session of Congress on March 12, 1947, President Harry Truman urges aid for Greece and Turkey.—Wide World

cans had charged the Communist-dominated government of Poland with a policy of "suppression, intimidation and coercion," which violated the solemn pledges given at the Potsdam and Yalta conferences.

On March 12, 1947, President Truman announced an unprecedented step that came to be called the Truman Doctrine. The United States, the President said, would extend economic and military aid to Greece and Turkey to help them maintain their independence. It was the first of many important steps on the long road ahead for the United States in the Cold War. It had happened because the British, the historic protectors of Greece, were exhausted by the long war and were unable even to support themselves. The British Foreign Office informed the United States that Britain must withdraw from Greece. Greece, torn by civil war between the Communists and non-Communists, needed American help if the story of Yugoslavia were not to be repeated.

No less important was the problem of bolstering Turkey. Turkey's strategic location—as the land and sea bridge between Europe and Asia—made it imperative that Turkey remain free from Communist domination. The Turks are a tough people, used to facing up to the threats of their huge neighbor to the north, Soviet Russia. But in this David-versus-Goliath struggle, all the advantage was with the threatening Soviets.

President Truman, in his speech announcing United States aid to Greece and Turkey, summed up the Truman Doctrine in two short sentences:

". . . it must be the policy of the United States to support free peoples who are resisting subjugation by armed minorities or by outside pressures. . . . We must assist free peoples to work out their own destinies in their own way.

Redeeming this pledge would lead American soldiers, technicians, diplomats, and citizens to the far corners of the globe.

"Warmongering!" thundered the Soviet Union in furious reaction to the Truman Doctrine. The men in the Kremlin could see that the American President's words had a far broader meaning than a simple pledge of aid to Greece and Turkey.

The next step came quickly and in an unlikely place—at

the graduation exercises of Harvard University in Cambridge, Massachusetts. The new American Secretary of State, George Catlett Marshall, spoke words that are among the most momentous in the history of mankind: Standing ramrod stiff, Marshall, the former Army Chief of Staff, master strategist of American victory in the Second World War, outlined a bold new global strategy of the Cold War. It came to be called the Marshall Plan. He said:

Europe's requirements . . . of food and other essential products—principally from America—are so much greater than her present ability to pay that she must have substantial additional help, or face economic, social and political deterioration.

Speaking in a low monotone, hardly ever glancing up from his prepared script, the new Secretary of State paid scant attention to the proud graduates and their beaming parents. George Catlett Marshall was speaking to the whole world, and he did not want to make any mistakes by departing from the text of his speech. General Marshall reviewed the situation in Europe. Allied-occupied West Germany was a jungle of rubble, unable to feed its people. Its businesses were in ruins, its factories bombed out or removed by the Russians. France was devastated. Everywhere in Europe was chaos and near-famine. Only the United States could effectively help, declared the man more famous as a five-star general than as a diplomat. Marshall said:

In considering the requirements for the rehabilitation of Europe, the physical loss of life, the . . . destruction of cities, factories, mines and railroads was correctly estimated . . . but the visible destruction was probably less serious than the dislocation of the entire fabric of European economy . . . Long-standing commercial ties, banks, insurance companies and shipping companies have disappeared. In many countries confidence in the local currency has been severely shaken.

Raw materials and fuel are in short supply. Machinery is lacking or worn out. The farmer . . . cannot find the goods for sale which he desires to purchase . . .

Aware that there were many Americans who thought this was "none of America's business," Secretary of State Marshall said:

The consequences to the economy of the United States should be apparent to all. . . . the United States should do whatever it is able to do to assist in the return of normal economic health in the world, without which there can be no political stability and no assured peace.

In the storm of Congressional debate that would arise over the Marshall Plan, the question would be asked over and over again: *Could* America live in peace and prosperity if there were chaos and ruin in Europe? And what if the Soviet Union made good its boast that the Red Army would "march to the sea?" In years to come, the great mines and factories of Western Europe, added to those of the Communist bloc, could easily tip the balance of international power against the United States. Opponents who hotly argued against "pouring any more American money down the European rathole" were overwhelmed in the final vote in both houses of Congress.

George Catlett Marshall, wearing beneath his academic robes a light tan suit that newspaper reporters commented looked very much like an Army officer's uniform without brass buttons, concluded his epochal speech with both a promise and a warning:

"Any government that is willing to assist in the task of recovery will find full cooperation . . . on the part of the United States . . ." he said. (The Marshall Plan was framed so that it would not exclude the nations of Eastern Europe, even the Soviet Union.) That was the promise—help to any country that would cooperate in the effort toward full recovery and a peaceful world.

Next came the warning:

"Any government which maneuvers to block the recovery of other nations cannot expect help from us," Marshall said bluntly. That was a notice to Soviet saboteurs. The warning grew more explicit: "Governments, political parties or groups which seek to perpetuate human misery in order to profit therefrom politically or otherwise will encounter the opposition of the United States.

It was a short speech, spoken quietly and in a mild voice, but the Marshall Plan was destined to have earthshaking impact.

Abruptly, the Marshall Plan did two things: first, it brought matters to a head in Europe by ending all polite fictions that the United States and the Soviet Union were still, somehow, partners. The wartime ties were severed neatly. Second, the Marshall plan, for the first time, took the United States off the defensive in Europe. For two years, the United States had mainly reacted to Soviet threats. (Typical was the Truman Doctrine, which gave aid to threatened Greece and Turkey in defense against Soviet-backed guerrilla warfare and subversion. Even George Kennan's containment theory was essentially defensive.)

Now, the United States proposed to take positive steps to preserve a free Europe.

The threat was very real. The Communist bloc was held together by the creation of a network of alliances comprising 23 treaties. The threat was not limited to Communist-bloc treaties only. The Soviet Union had massive armed forces amounting to a staggering 200 divisions, or between 240,000 and 400,000 troops, plus the manpower of its satellites. On the other hand, the democratic nations of Europe had demobilized most of their armies, were weak from the ruin of war, and Communist parties were working hard to undermine recovery from inside. An alliance of the free nations was clearly needed.

The Marshall Plan was the first step.

It is important to take a quick look at the work of George C. Marshall as secretary of state. Marshall proved, in some ways, to be the most surprising American secretary of state in a century. When he took office, some observers had open reservations about the wisdom of a military man holding the United States' top diplomatic post. *Newsweek* magazine, for instance, reported that most of Marshall's top assistants moved right over to State from the Pentagon, the nation's defense headquarters. Every member of his personal staff still called Marshall "General," *Newsweek* reported. Others wrote, not entirely approvingly, that Marshall "shook up" the State Department by organizing a Policy Planning Committee copied from military organization.

Marshall paid no heed to his critics. This tight-lipped, soft-spoken Virginian had made military history by coming from Virginia Military Institute instead of West Point and becoming

53

Chief of Staff. The great military strategist had learned well the important lesson that good intentions, without adequate programs and military support, were not likely to go far in the merciless competition with the Russians.

From the standpoint of history, many top experts now credit George C. Marshall with revitalizing the State Department. Secretary of State Dean Rusk, for example, in an interview with the authors, termed Marshall one of the five greatest secretaries of state ever to hold that enormously sensitive and demanding post. Marshall selected the brilliant George Kennan to head the Policy Planning Committee, and this body has, over the years, made important contributions to American foreign policy.

The blunt truth was that, until the advent of George Marshall as secretary of state, the Department had been performing poorly in the great crisis of the Cold War. Secretary of State Cordell Hull and President Franklin Roosevelt had never worked closely. F.D.R., some experts hint, would have been happy had Mr. Hull seen fit to resign. When he did not, F.D.R. got into the habit of bypassing the State Department, using roving ambassadors unconnected with the Department for the highest missions of state, and often failing to inform the State Department of things that properly fell within its province. Secretary of State Edward Stettinius, who succeeded Hull, served only briefly. Secretary of State James F. Byrnes, next on the list, was able, but a personality clash developed between him and President Truman. Marshall was the first strong secretary of state in many years who also enjoyed the absolute confidence of his chief, the president. Harry S. Truman was fond of calling Marshall "the greatest living American." Marshall's prestige, grasp of military and strategic concepts, and administrative ability reenergized the State Department. The improvement of the Western response to Soviet challenges owes much to George C. Marshall.

Soviet bitterness at the Marshall Plan quickly emerged into the open. Newspaper readers the world over were startled, on September 19, 1947, by an account of the United Nations session at its temporary quarters, at Lake Success, N.Y. The Soviet Union's Andrei Vyshinsky, infamous as a prosecutor at Stalin's purge trials and a former ambassador to the United

States, cut loose with a stinging denunciation of many prominent Americans—by name.

Among the "warmongers" Vyshinsky singled out with special violence was an American delegate to the United Nations, John Foster Dulles. Dulles had long been prominent in legal and diplomatic circles but was not widely known by the American public at that time. (Later he was to become possibly the most powerful and controversial American secretary of state in the nation's history.)

The incident marked the beginning of something new in American foreign policy, a bipartisan approach, in which members of both the Democratic and Republican parties took part. Presidents Roosevelt and Truman, well remembering the experience of President Woodrow Wilson after World War I, took pains to have prominent Republicans play a role in foreign affairs. President Wilson had advocated a League of Nations, but made the political mistake of taking only leading Democrats to the Peace Conference with him. This angered the Republicans who dominated the United States Senate, which must approve by a two-thirds majority any treaties to which the United States is a party. The Senate rejected the Versailles Treaty of World War I and refused to consent to America's joining the League of Nations.

Democratic Presidents Roosevelt and Truman, wishing to avoid the problems that had frustrated President Wilson after the first World War, had brought numerous Republicans into prominent roles in foreign affairs during the early Cold War period. The nation must "close ranks," and "politics must stop at the water's edge"—so went the saying that quickly became a cliché. This united front on foreign affairs was to add much to America's strength, enabling it to move quickly and decisively to meet threats posed by the Communists.

The most prominent Republican in the immediate postwar period was United States Senator Arthur Vandenberg of Michigan. The election of 1946 gave the Republicans a majority in the Senate, automatically making Vandenberg chairman of the Foreign Relations Committee of the Senate. This involved heavy duties, so Senator Vandenberg relinquished his place as a delegate to the United Nations. By the time Vyshinsky made his free-swinging attack at the United Nations, Dulles was the principle Republican spokesman in American foreign affairs.

In his unprecedented (and undiplomatic) attack, Russia's Vyshinsky attacked the prominent Americans, including Dulles, as "war propagandists . . . afraid of an economic crisis," and as men who were "instigating a new war as a means of preventing the approaching menace and collapse of their profits."

The Russian delegate denounced the Truman Doctrine and the Marshall Plan as "simply attempts to subjugate European countries to U. S. economic monopolies."

This view of the United States was taken from the views of Karl Marx and Nikolai Lenin, the Communist oracles, of "capitalist wars" as a kind of murder for profit by large monopolies who reaped huge fortunes from war.

Dulles, who was listening while Vyshinsky spoke, replied with a denunciation of "Soviet Expansion" and "territorial seizure" of Eastern European nations. That added fuel to the fire of Vyshinsky's fury and, for the next two weeks, a running verbal duel raged between the American and the Russian. It was notable for revealing a glaring weakness in the United Nations' ability to keep the peace, plus an ingenious American plan for overcoming this weakness.

A week after his first attack, Vyshinsky resumed the offensive. He denounced "warmongers" who "advocated war" against "peace-loving nations" like the Soviet Union. In near-hysteria, he again singled out Dulles, shouting: "Mr. Dulles instigates a policy toward the U. S. S. R. which cannot but lead to war!" He climaxed his tirade by stating that Dulles and "other warmongers" should be "thrown in chains."

Vyshinsky's strong words had an effect exactly the opposite of what the Soviet delegate had no doubt intended. Millions of Americans who had never before heard of John Foster Dulles became aware of him, and the attack enhanced his role in United States foreign policy.

In the violent debate, Vyshinsky said that American proposals for a "little Assembly plan" were an attempt to "steamroller" the United Nations. According to the Russian delegate the plan would transform the General Assembly, in which all nations were represented, into the most important part of the international organization, whereas the Charter quite clearly provided that the Security Council should be the most important. It was quite true that the United States was pressing hard for an increase in the role of the General Assembly in the United Nations. Otherwise, the United Nations would have been almost entirely impotent. The Soviet Union from the first showed quite plainly that it would use its veto in the Security Council to stop action on anything the United Nations tried to do that the Soviet Union did not like. In the General Assembly, there was no Soviet veto. If the United Nations were to function at all in the face of strong disagreement between the superpowers —the Soviet Union and the United States—it would be through the action of the General Assembly, not the Security Council.

One of the casualties of the Cold War was the hope that the United Nations could keep the peace all by itself. In the years to come, the United Nations would prove a useful means of damping down "small wars" in the Middle East and elsewhere. But in a direct clash between the superpowers, the United Nations lacks the power for decisive action.

George Kennan, who conceived the United States' containment policy toward the Soviet Union, also commented: "The towers of the Kremlin cast a long shadow." That "long shadow" is reflected in local Communist parties in every nation of the world. The Kremlin's power was increased, on October 5, 1947, at a clandestine meeting in Poland—supposedly top secret, but of which news leaked to the outside world. The "Communist International" (the Comintern) was abolished. A new, better financed, more aggressive organization, the Cominform, was set up in the shadowy Communist world that is part politics, part sabotage and subversion. It would play a vital role in the Cold War, fomenting trouble in scores of nations. It was particularly dangerous from 1947 to 1953, because all reigns of power led directly to the Kremlin—to Josef Stalin, "the Man of Steel." The Master of Russia was strong enough to tolerate no competitors to his power in the Soviet Union, or in any of the Communist parties in any other country, either.

As 1947 drew to a close, shattering headlines smashed the last comfortable illusion of the American people—a feeling that all would be well, because, in spite of everything, "We have got

Chapter Seven

TRAGEDY IN CZECHOSLOVAKIA, CRISIS IN BERLIN, AND HOPE IN THE BALKANS

"It is our heart's desire that peace may be preserved, but we should by now have learned that there is no safety in yielding to dictators whether Nazi or Communist."
—Winston Churchill, 1948

In late December, 1947, President Harry Truman signed into law bills designed to provide economic assistance to the war-wrecked economies of France, Italy, and Austria under the widening scope of the Marshall Plan. The ink was barely dry when a successful Communist coup d'état exploded in the heart of Central Europe. The coup, an illegal but bloodless Communist takeover in Czechoslovakia, shook the Western allies.

The dramatic coup, under the leadership of Czech Premier Klement Gottwald, was an "overnight" surprise. In the free elections held in Czechoslovakia in 1946, only 38 percent of the voters elected 114 Communist Assembly Deputies out of the total of 300, achieving a plurality among the many political parties. Nevertheless the shock waves produced by the Communist takeover in Czechoslovakia were profound. In contrast to the other countries of Eastern Europe, Czechoslovakia had been a true democracy before the war. It was the first highly industrialized country to "adopt" Communism—albeit with the help of terror. If Communism could come "peaceably," in the heartland of Central Europe, to a literate and industrialized people, where, many wondered, would it strike next?

Czechoslovakia had not suffered devastating bombing during World War II. The nation's industry was intact, but the Czech people, who had lived under the murderous Nazi occupation, were tired—169,000 Czechs out of a population of 12 million had been executed during the Hitler reign of terror. The small Bohemian village of Lidice, for example, had been erased from the map in savage reprisal for the assassination of Nazi leader Reinhard Heydrich. All its men were killed and its women and children deported as slave laborers. The brutal liquidation of the little town made Lidice a concept in modern vocabularies as the destruction of Carthage had been in the ancient world.

With the Communist coup of February 24, 1948, new faces came to the fore in the Cold War—faces virtually unknown outside Czechoslovakia. Klement Gottwald, a carpenter by trade and a Catholic by birth, was installed as president of Czechoslovakia by the Archbishop of Prague—the country's leading

Czechoslovakian Communists gather in Prague's Old Town Square on February 21, 1948, in support of Premier Klement Gottwald's seizure of power.—Wide World

Catholic dignitary. Though a Communist, Gottwald was considered a political moderate, and he had served in the prewar Czech Republic's Parliament. Prime Minister Antonin Zapotocky fitted the routine Communist-leadership mold more precisely. Zapotocky, son of a Socialist leader who had been imprisoned for many years, served a considerable amount of time in jail for labor agitation prior to World War II. A stonemason by trade, he went to Moscow as a left-wing representative of the Czech Social Democratic Party and was converted to Communism. On his return to Prague, the Czech capital, Zapotocky became a union organizer.

Both able men, Gottwald and Zapotocky would wrench the considerable Czech economy away from the manufacturing of consumer goods toward that of heavy industry. In pre-World War II days, the Czech industrial output had traditionally been oriented toward the West. Pottery, textiles, toys, beer, and luxury goods went to Western markets. The new Czech economy, however, was soon geared to the production of heavy machinery and steel—much of it for use in the Sovietized world of the East—and its important production was added to that of the Communist bloc.

Upon the Communist takeover, the Iron Curtain slammed down immediately, imprisoning the Czechs trapped by their new masters. On March 13, 1948, an escapee who reached Hof, West Germany, reported that Czechoslovakia's new "socialist" masters were sentencing captured would-be escapees to terms ranging from five to twenty years in prison.

Close on the heels of the Czech disaster came rumblings of trouble in Berlin. Late in March, 1948, Russia's Vassily D. Sokolovsky, Commander of the Russian Zone of divided Berlin, rose from the Control Council table and announced to the other Allied administrators: "The Control Council no longer exists as an organ of government."

With these dramatic words, prepared in advance of the meeting, the handsome, heavy-set marshal and his sixteen-man team took a familiar "Russian walk."

With the Russian walkout, the point of no return was reached in Berlin. Until then, in theory at least, Berlin was still a unified city, jointly ruled by the "Big Four" powers—the United States, Britain, France, and the Soviet Union. Now, even the remnants of the ineffective Control Commission had been wiped out.

The Western powers responded by a union of the British and American zones of occupation (later to be joined by the French Zone), which laid the foundations of the present Federal Republic of Germany.

The Russians set demands before the Control Council members and later, on March 30, 1949, formal Soviet provisions were given to the Western governments: 1) United States (and all Allied) personnel traveling through the Soviet Zone were to present documentary evidence of identity to Soviet personnel. 2) All military freight traveling across the Soviet Zone into and out of Berlin was to be checked through Soviet checkpoints. 3) There was to be inspection by the Soviet authorities of all baggage of personnel traveling through the Soviet Zone.

Maj. General Charles Kenon Gailey, Jr., the Chief of Staff of the United States Military Government, promptly told the Russians that their provisions were "unacceptable" and that "such unilateral changes of policy could not be recognized."

In London and Washington, the Russian move in Berlin was noted grimly. United States Secretary of State George Marshall immediately announced: "The United States intends to continue to fulfill its responsibilities as a member of the Control Council and *as a joint occupant to the city of Berlin*." [Authors' italics.] Harold MacMillan, the leader of His Majesty's loyal Opposition in the House of Commons, said: "We must face the risk of war."

The Allied governments ignored the Soviet provisions. April 1, 1948, was the deadline date set by the Soviets for compliance or a "blockade" of the city of Berlin. On that day two United States and two British trains en route to Berlin were turned back at the border of the Soviet Zone of Occupation, 110 miles to the west.

April 1 marked the beginning of the Soviet Union's formal drive to push the Allied powers out of West Berlin. It set the stage for the widening arena of the Cold War. Later in the month, the Soviets even stopped international train service to Berlin! By early May, 1948, Russian military officers no longer attended the meetings of the Allied Kommandatura for the administration of the city. Later, in the summer, after maneuvers and countermeasures by the Allies, the Soviets removed the huge portrait of Stalin and the Soviet flag from the Kommandatura building—a final gesture symbolizing the complete breakdown of the four-power control in Berlin.

For nearly three months, the Soviets played a "cat and mouse" game with the West—and with the fate of Berliners. Restrictions on travel were imposed and then removed. Freight routes were ordered changed. Finally, freight could be shipped only via one route—Helmstedt—for "technical" reasons, the Soviets said. Meanwhile, a fierce propaganda barrage filled the Communist press, directed at all of Berlin. The Communist *Berliner-Zeitung* reported that there would be an "unavoidable withdrawal of the Allies, which will come about very suddenly—within the near future."

There was a tremendous dispute over currency reform. The Communists attempted to bully the West Berlin City Assembly. Over and over Soviet propaganda hammered at one theme: the Western powers would be forced out of Berlin.

The thin, lined face and piercing dark eyes of General Lucius Clay, United States Commander in Berlin, soon became familiar to Americans and appeared in newspapers around the world. Clay was America's man on the scene in a series of daring—and unexpected—moves to continue to supply besieged West Berlin, an island of freedom 110 miles deep in a Communist sea. Food, fuel, and the necessities of life would be brought in by airlift. Could a huge city be fed just by flown-in supplies? The Communists doubted it. Another crisis gripped the world. Would the Communists interfere with the airlift? That would mean war.

In a message to Washington concerning the worsening Berlin situation, Clay said:

> We should not leave Berlin unless driven out by force. . . . We have lost Czechoslovakia. Norway is threatened. We retreat from Berlin. When Berlin falls, Western Germany will be next. . . . If we withdraw our position in Europe is threatened. If America does not understand this now, does not know the issue is cast, then it never will, and Communism will run rampant. I believe the future of democracy requires us to stay.

Clay, a career Army officer, had been graduated from West

Point in 1918 as an Army engineer. He had held many high administrative positions that ideally prepared him for the current challenge. In 1940–41 Clay had directed the first national civil airport program in the United States. He had been head of Army Procurement. Later Clay would serve as commander of war mobilization—the difficult job of conversion to war. When he first went to Germany he had been its deputy military commander, and in 1947 he had become Commander in Chief of all United States Forces and Military Governor of the United States Zone in Germany, with headquarters in Berlin. It was here, then, in Berlin, in the spring of 1948, that the lines of the Cold War hardened into ominous reality. At stake was Germany and the possible unity of that hungry, impoverished country, which was beginning to emerge from the complete devastation of the war.

The peace of the world, plus the "credibility" of the West's warnings to the Russians that it would defend, and not be driven out of, Germany were at stake. The decision was made to fight, if necessary, to uphold the basic human and political freedoms of democracy. However, if possible, it was decided not to fight but to stay put and outlast the Soviets in the war of will and nerves. The Soviet blockade of Berlin was widely recognized as another test. To fail this test would mean far more than just the loss of West Berlin—though Berlin was the most important manufacturing city in Germany. It would encourage the cocky Russians to further aggressions, and it would terrorize opponents of Communism.

One of the biggest Soviet aims of the Berlin blockade went beyond Berlin—to snuff out the Marshall Plan before it could become effective. If the United States' shield could not protect Berlin, could it protect West Germany, France, Belgium, Holland, or any other country in Western Europe?

Stalin's Berlin blockade was a challenge that had to be met. And, for a year, it would bring the world close to the brink. A false step on either side might lead to war.

But not all the trouble in the world in the spring of 1948 was of Russian making. In Yugoslavia, little noticed except in the world of the diplomats, an important crack was being made in the Kremlin Wall. It came out into the open in March, 1948, with a letter from Yugoslavia's Communist dictator, Marshal

Tito, to Soviet Foreign Minister V. M. Molotov, protesting the recall of Soviet advisers and military specialists from Yugoslavia. And it began something brand new in the Communist world—a show of independence on the part of what the Soviets fondly thought was a subservient satellite country.

The newly "elected" Premier Tito of the Federal People's Republic of Yugoslavia followed the pattern of many of the other "People's Republics" that were being formed and solidified in Eastern Europe. But there were several vital distinctions that would continue throughout the long years of the Cold War and would place Communist Yugoslavia in a special position. Tito enjoyed immense popular support and popularity in his own country. His rule had not been imposed on the people in the way, for example, that Walter Ulbricht's was in East Germany —by Soviet tanks and bayonets. Tito was the hero of his country, a man regarded as the personification of a united Yugoslavian state. He did not depend upon Stalin's Red Army to keep him in power.

To people who regarded one Communist country as exactly like another, the difference was not apparent. But, from the first, Tito disturbed the Kremlin with his independence. And, in 1948, he slammed the door shut hard on Greek Communist guerrillas who were in the habit of fighting in Greece when the odds were in their favor, then dodging back over the Communist border when loyal Greek armies appeared. As his differences with the Kremlin increased, Tito denied the Greek Communists refuge in Yugoslavia and that helped insure victory for the West in the Greek civil war.

By June, 1948, the very word "Communist" had been stretched into an elastic label by the independent Tito. One astonished writer said, after visiting Yugoslavia, that they engaged in practices "almost as Democratic as a New England town meeting and as capitalistic as a flint-eyed Missouri banker!"

This comment was much too strong, perhaps. But there is no doubt that the Yugoslavs were very trying to Josef Stalin.

Meanwhile, all over Europe, the Cold War was approaching a crisis. Could the Marshall Plan stave off the Soviet threat? Would the blockade drive the Western powers from Berlin? And what would happen in the quarrel between Tito and Stalin?

Chapter Eight

BERLIN BLOCKADE

"We shall sit tight. We will not be provocative. . . . Evacuation to me is unthinkable. . . ."
—General Lucius D. Clay, 1948

The battle lines, after weeks of moves, counter moves, and negotiations, were drawn in Berlin in the dawn hours of June 24, 1948. The Soviet Government imposed a total blockade on the city of Berlin. Orders were issued to Soviet troops at the East German border that no movement of supplies would be permitted into the Western Sector of the city, 110 miles inside East Germany.

The Soviets intended one of two grim courses for the Western forces and the people of Berlin—starvation or surrender. The Berlin blockade was ruthless. No movement of food meant hunger, because except for little garden plots within the huge perimeter of the city, all of Berlin's food came in from outside. The little cabbage patches and vegetable gardens were utterly incapable of feeding the two million persons in the Western Sector. Berlin's exposed position gave the Communists every advantage. Every pound of coal, every quart of milk, every pair of shoes, every bit of raw material for factories had to be brought across hostile territory controlled by the Ulbricht government, which had vowed to destroy freedom in Berlin.

General Clay reports in *Decision in Germany*:

I thought that the extension of the blockade to cut food off from the German population in Berlin might succeed in forcing us out, but I doubted if the Russians would be so foolish as to make a move which would alienate the German population completely."

In pre-Hitler days Berlin had been a city with the largest Communist party in the world after Moscow. Germany was the home country of both Marx and Engels.

The Communists, in spite of their crushing rebuff in the 1946 elections, still hopefully said that "Communism was as German as sauerkraut."

Time would prove otherwise.

The Soviet Union claimed that there were no written agreements providing for Allied access to Berlin. The Western powers hotly maintained that access to the besieged city was a part of their right to be in the city as occupying powers under the wartime agreements.

The questions of lines of communication and of the importation of food and coal supplies into Berlin had been raised and discussed at the June 29, 1945, meeting of the representatives of the Allied commands. Agreements had been reached and approved by all four powers of the Control Council for the administration of Berlin by September 10, 1945, followed by agreements establishing air corridors to and from Berlin. The agreements specified that "aircraft of the occupying powers might at any time make use of three corridors, of a width of twenty English miles each . . . one toward Hamburg, one toward Buckeburg, and a third toward Frankfurt."

In other agreements on Berlin, it had been clearly established that *all* Berlin would be administered by the four occupying powers. Berlin was thus an international enclave and was never considered as an area, part of, or on the territory of the Soviet Zone of occupation.

Clearly, the Soviet blockade of Berlin violated these earlier agreements. It soon became evident that the Soviet Union was attempting to include as part of the Soviet Zone the former German capital city—Berlin.

The Soviet actions were, in part, a retaliation against the new currency reform for the Western zones of Germany introduced by the two Allied powers and, in part, a protest and propaganda move to stall the possibility of the formation of a federation of West Germany as discussed at the London Six-Power Conference in February, 1948.

The February London Conference was called to try and solve some of the most pressing problems of Germany and to attempt to "put an end to a state of uncertainty and economic deterioration in Germany which threatens recovery in all of Europe," a note to the Soviet Government from the United States State Department reported.

When the 1947 London Conference of the quadripartite Council of Foreign Ministers failed to produce agreement on the establishment of a central German administration, the three Western powers entered into what are called the "London Agreements," concluded on June 1, 1947, resolving to let the Western German people establish a basis for a democratic form of government.

The propaganda moves the Soviet Government made at this time are interesting. In the Russian Zone of occupation, an attempt was made to get 12,000,000 German signatures for an "all German Unity" government and to protest against the formation of the democratic-inspired West German Federal Union.

A huge sign in East Berlin read:

ATTENTION

YOU ARE NOW ENTERING THE AMERICAN SECTOR. AMERICAN DEMOCRACY RULES THERE. THEY WANT TO FORBID THE WILL OF THE PEOPLE. BUT NO POWER IN THE WORLD CAN FORBID YOU TO SIGN. DON'T BE ROBBED OF YOUR FUNDAMENTAL DEMOCRATIC RIGHTS. SIGN UP HERE.

The introduction of new currency by the Western powers was imperative to save West German economic recovery. The Soviet boycott of the Berlin Control Council meetings prevented a four-power discussion of currency reform for the whole of Germany as originally planned by the Allies.

On June 18, 1948, General Sir Brian Robertson of the Berlin Kommandatura wrote a letter to the Soviet Zone commandant, Marshal Sokolovsky, which aptly states the necessity for currency reform.

The British Zone is suffering acutely from the evils of inflation and economic stagnation which our quadripartite proposals for financial reform were designed long ago to eradicate, and I feel that I am not justified in waiting any longer before taking remedial measures.

I have therefore decided to include the British Zone in a scheme of currency reform to be introduced into the Western Zones on Sunday, June 20th.

The British Sector of Berlin will remain unaffected by this decision. I recognize the special circumstances of quadripartite government in Berlin and have no wish to disturb it, *unless it becomes unavoidable.* [Authors' italics.]

The Allied response to the Berlin blockade was the Berlin airlift. Two days after the imposition of the Soviet blockade of the city, the Western allied forces, operating under the leadership of General Clay, then Germany's military governor, and General Curtis LeMay, Commander of the Air Forces in Germany, began flying food and other essential supplies into Tempelhof and Gatow airports. Both airports were in West Berlin. But, hemmed in by homes and buildings, the small landing strips were soon being taxed to the utmost to handle the never-ending stream of big cargo planes that soon began to drone in, one landing almost as soon as the one before it had turned off the runway.

West Berliners watch as a plane loaded with supplies prepares to land during the Soviet blockade of 1948–49.—U.S. Department of State

The big cargo planes were stripped for action as freight cars. Any passengers coming to Berlin—military personnel, newsmen covering the story, even high-ranking diplomats—rode "steerage," crowding in alongside sacks of potatoes, bulk coal, and crates of dismantled machinery that were needed to keep Berlin alive.

The fantastic airlift, variously called Operation Vittles and Operation Plainfare, began simply enough when General Clay in Berlin picked up his telephone and called General LeMay in Wiesbaden, 280 miles away. And the "impossible" was accomplished.

Before the end of the Berlin blockade almost a year later, on May 12, 1949, the massive total of 2,343,302 tons of food and essential supplies would be delivered by air! More than 226,000 flights were made, creating a fantastic *Luftbrücke* ("air bridge") from the West. Commercial planes, such as those of the fledgling Alaska Airways, as well as heavy-duty military craft would be pressed into service. The entire 48th Troop Carrier Squadron based in Texas would be called into action, as well as the 20th from far-off Panama and the 54th based in Alaska. All went on round-the-clock air freight duty. A new airport, Tegel, would be built in the French Sector, with equipment dismantled in the West, flown over by the *Luftbrücke,* and then put back together in Berlin by hand labor.

The two resourceful generals, Clay and LeMay, would soon add a third general to their team—Air Force General William Turner, the man who had organized the remarkable airlift over the "Hump" in Southeast Asia during World War II.

Berlin's postage-stamp airfields presented a grim challenge to continuous air movement. Tempelhof and Gatow would clock aircraft landing and taking off every three minutes! "A mass operation of the present scale in the Berlin airspace presents the trickiest traffic problem that aviation has yet produced," declared General Turner.

Skilled and courageous pilots faced many hazards. Flying in air corridors only twenty miles wide, harried by considerable "buzzing" of the air lanes by Soviet planes (which would "dart out of nowhere," as one pilot reported), and landing with startling accuracy almost to the second, to keep the precise schedules at Gatow and Tempelhof—only a scant eleven air miles apart—

proved dangerous. Thirty-six British and American airmen died in crashes in the first six months of the Berlin airlift.

As the months wore on, the airlift became a symbol of just how resourceful a people can be if they must. At first the Communists greeted the Western effort to supply two million people with food, fuel, and other necessities by air as incredible, if not simply impossible. *Neues Deutschland,* the official newspaper of the Communist Socialist Unity Party (the SED) in East Berlin, ridiculed the attempt. "The airlift is meaningless," *Neues Deutschland* said and went on to explain that it could not possibly succeed.

To maintain the demanding precision schedules for supplying the city, particularly as winter began to close in, the airlift planes' flying directions included a new hazard—flying at staggered altitudes within the narrow 20-mile-wide corridors of the *Luftbrücke.* It meant, too, flying in thick fog, sleet, and blinding snow—weather no commercial flights would contend with. And the courageous pilots were not allowed to fly above their designated altitudes to avoid storms. By Christmas the airlift had accomplished the considerable task of delivering 700,000 tons of supplies. The flights were clocked into Berlin at 550 daily, with an average of 3,800 tons of supplies delivered per day.

Berlin was a grim, sick city in the cold winter of 1948. Electricity was rationed due to short fuel supplies. The city was "blacked out" from sundown to sunrise. Some 3,500 Berlin business firms shut down, and 5,000 others operated on half-day schedules to save precious power. After sundown all public transportation ceased. Private homes throughout the city were without the precious coal needed for heat.

Once more the woodmen's axes rang through the few streets where trees still grew and in the rapidly depleted forests along the city's riverbanks. The once-luxurient trees, the pride of prewar Berlin, were once again needed to provide heat for the shivering city.

A typically generous offshoot of the airlift was something nicknamed "Operation Little Vittles," started by Allied servicemen. Since only essentials could be carried (most of the food was dehydrated first to save cargo space), children rarely found any luxuries on their tables at home. "Operation Little Vittles" attempted to make the airlift a holiday adventure for the *kinder* (children). Pilots started the project, and soon far-off cities in America contributed. Mobile, Alabama, for example, rose to the call of one pilot, Lieutenant Gale Halverson, by sending an initial shipment of 500 pounds of handkerchiefs to aid the resourceful pilots. They turned these into miniature parachutes, filled them with donations of chocolate bars and gumdrops and dropped the tiny packages of goodies over the city as the planes came roaring in for a landing.

Special American holidays were celebrated by the airmen with extra quotas of supplies. On Air Force Day, September 16, 1948, the total of supplies was raised to 7,000 tons. On George Washington's Birthday, February 22, 1949, the tonnage rose to well over 7,000 tons.

Today a monument to the brave and generous airmen of the *Luftbrücke* stands at Tempelhof Airport in West Berlin. It was erected by the grateful people of Berlin and commemorates the Allied flyers who gave their lives so that the people of the city could live.

The airlift staved off possible war by avoiding the clash of troops that might have been needed to "fight through" trains and trucks. The Soviets harassed Allied pilots but did not shoot any airplanes down. That would have left Britain, France, and the United States with no alternative but to fight.

The Berlin blockade had a lasting—and important—effect. It backfired against the Communists. By turns, the Communists tried terror, threats, and even bribes and blandishments to win over the people of West Berlin. All failed. "Berlin has a new common bond of shared courage," one correspondent wrote at the time, and it soon led to a new bond between the people of West Berlin and the West.

World events swept on even as the Berlin airlift was defying Stalin's Berlin blockade. Both a dramatic triumph and a dramatic defeat now faced the free world. March, 1949, saw the signing of the North Atlantic Treaty—perhaps the single most important step taken by the Western nations in the Cold War, since it united them in a common defense.

Elsewhere the news was disastrous. The Communists were scoring stunning victories in China.

Chapter Nine

RED TIDES OF FORTUNE IN THE FAR EAST

"Lenin never regarded the Republic of the Soviets as an end in itself. To him it was always a link needed to strengthen the chain of revolutionary movement in the countries of the East and West, a link needed to facilitate the victory of the working people over capitalism."

—Josef Stalin, *Pravda,*
January 30, 1924

In January, 1949, the Chinese People's Liberation Army accepted the surrender of one of the foremost Nationalist Chinese generals, Fu Tso-yi, who had valiantly fought the Japanese in World War II. It was then that the victorious Communist troops of Mao Tse-tung's Red Army marched into China's ancient "Celestial Capital," Peking. In the victorious Red Chinese columns were hundreds of American tanks and much other American Army military stock that had been captured or obtained by bribe from the retreating Kuomintang forces led by Nationalist leader Chiang Kai-shek. An eyewitness, Derk Bodde, writing in his *Peking Diary,* reports, "It was primarily a display of American military equipment."

By October 1, 1949, the Chinese People's Republic had been proclaimed. A "Bamboo Curtain" came down on the ancient state of China. The victorious Communist, Mao Tse-tung, announced a "new democracy," and China was torn asunder and put upon the path toward becoming a "Sovietized socialized state."

The bitter aftermath of the second World War in China had led to even more bitter and agonizing civil war. Mao's Communist forces sought to overthrow the militarily and numerically superior forces of Generalissimo Chiang Kai-shek. In one of history's most stunning chapters, Mao succeeded, helped by Nationalist corruption, incompetence, and demoralization of troops, as well as raging inflation inside China, and disaffection by the Chinese peasants.

In 1949, the balance of power in Asia was shifted dramatically in the Communists' favor as Chiang's forces fled from the mainland of China to the island of Formosa (Taiwan).

As early as October 30, 1948, the Chinese Communists had won control of all Manchuria by capturing Mukden, the last Nationalist stronghold. Six weeks later, on January 14, 1949, the Communist troops had captured Tientsin. A week after that Peking (Peiping) fell. The Communists reached the bank of the Yangtze River and Mao Tse-tung demanded the "unconditional surrender" of Chiang Kai-shek. The agony of the Chinese civil war would be prolonged until December 8, 1949, when the final Nationalist flight from Chengtu to Formosa ended the long struggle. At almost every step, the Nationalists had been outgeneraled and out-fought. Above all, Chiang's forces lost the contest for the loyalty of the Chinese peasant. In an ancient land where peasants numbered nine people out of every ten, that was decisive.

George Kennan, while a senior United States State Department official and veteran diplomat, wrote that it was not "Moscow, and least of all Washington, which really delivered China into the hands of the Communists. It was the Japanese."

For far more than China alone was at stake. The Communist victory in China imperiled all of Asia. To the south, for example, lay the sprawling French colony of Indochina. (We now know part of it as Vietnam). With the victory of Mao Tse-tung in China, world opinion was forced to look at the smoldering war going on in Vietnam between the forces of the Vietnamese general Ho Chi Minh and those of the French. And to the east, a peninsula of land jutted out like a thumb into the Sea of Japan. This land, like Vietnam, would soon become a battleground in the Cold War. It was Korea, divided into two zones, North and South. The United States refused to recognize Communist-held North Korea, because no free elections had ever been held there —a violation of post-war agreements. But it had accorded full diplomatic recognition to the Republic of Korea (the South) on January 1, 1949. Further to the east lay Japan, with whom no final treaty of peace had yet been made following the second World War. To the southwest were India and Pakistan, just concluding a cease-fire in their bitter, undeclared war over Kashmir.

All about the victorious Chinese Communists lay possibilities for new expansion of Communism. Just as the Communists were beginning to suffer their greatest defeats in Europe, they were beginning to enjoy their greatest postwar victories in Asia.

Indochina was later to assume special importance as one of the sites of the longest war in American history. Let us meet some new faces in the Cold War: Mao Tse-tung, poet, philosopher and expert on guerrilla warfare, who led the Red Chinese to victory; Chiang Kai-shek, his defeated Nationalist adversary; and a slender, philosopher-like figure named Ho Chi Minh, leader of Indochinese resistance against the French whose rule had been interrupted by the Japanese conquest of Indochina during the second World War.

In the vast land of China, it has often been said that the power to shape events, make decisions, and set forth goals generally becomes concentrated in the hands of one man. Mao Tse-tung, who dominated Chinese Communism from the late 1920's and later emerged as master of China, was such a man. Mao, the Chinese leader, exponent of the Marxist-Leninist philosophy, and one of the founders of the Chinese Communist Party, was born in the province of Hunan on December 26, 1893. He came to the Chinese capital of Peking as an impoverished young student and teacher. After the founding of the Chinese Communist Party in 1921, Mao spent years in organizational work in his native Hunan, where (surprisingly) he acted as a political adviser to both the Communists and the legal Kuomintang Government.

After the Kuomintang-Communist split in 1927, Mao led a successful revolt in his native Hunan province. He succeeded in winning over the majority of the peasants to his cause, and he established an effective Sovietized resistance organization there. Living in caves, moving constantly to avoid detection, Mao was able to organize cadres of hardened soldiers—the nucleus of the Chinese Red Army. In 1931, he was named chairman of the "Soviet Republic of China."

In 1934–35, Mao led his Red Army on the celebrated "long march" across the "rooftop" of China from Kiangsi province to

Yenan—6,000 miles! Mao and his troops fought in territory held by warlords or the hostile Nationalist Kuomintang. They lived off the land and always recruited the peasants to their revolutionary cause. Mao and his fellow Red Army leader, Chu Teh, led their troops against the Japanese—fighting savagely and simultaneously this invading enemy and "the enemy within," the Kuomintang armies of Chiang Kai-shek. All the while, the ranks of the Chinese Red Army grew, swollen with new recruits from the dispossessed peasantry.

After the second World War, Mao advocated a coalition government with the Kuomintang. But the two forces again split, and the long Chinese civil war resumed in 1946. Mao's forces again swelled with new recruits. With great skill, he used both force and persuasion to advance his revolutionary army under the banner of political Communism as a way of life. Despite incredible odds, and despite the fact that the Allies were supplying the armies of Chiang Kai-shek, the Mao forces were successful. After driving the Nationalists from the Chinese mainland, the Chinese People's Republic was founded.

Within Communist China, Mao is regarded not only as a great political leader and military strategist, but also as a teacher, poet, philosopher, and national savior and liberator—perhaps, interestingly, in the same way that Americans regard George Washington or South Americans think of Simon Bolívar.

Mao's writings are fascinating but somewhat out of date in the modern world—except on the subject of guerrilla warfare, a subject he mastered during the long march and the struggle for China. Mao's other writings depict the world in terms of 19th-century Marxist doctrine, as a ceaseless struggle between the toiling masses and their capitalistic "oppressors."

Mao understood well the need to know and become identified with the Chinese peasant: usually ignorant, and ravaged by disease. "Having become a Revolutionary, I found myself in the same ranks as the workers, peasants and soldiers in the Revolutionary Army," Mao once said in an interview. "It was then and only then that a fundamental change in the . . . feelings implanted in me by bourgeois schools took place."

Mao Tse-tung proved a brilliant military leader. His code has been to raise Communist China to the position of a world power —by force. He summed up this belief in a famous phrase: "All political power grows out of the barrel of a gun." Mao's impact was perhaps best summed up by author Edgar Snow in his book, *The Other Side Of The River:* "Generations of Western dominance in Asia had brought not peace but a sword . . . not until China learned to use modern weapons effectively did the West begin to respect her."

No one doubts that Communist China is a formidable power today.

Chiang Kai-shek, a decade older than Mao, was the son of a wealthy landowner. He came to power in China in 1928 when the Kuomintang seized control of the divided country—some of which was under the dissenting followers of Dr. Sun Yat-sen, the great Chinese republican revolutionary leader. Much of China was then under the domination of warlords—primarily semi-independent military commanders in the north. The Kuomintang established a government that was recognized by the outside world. But trouble continued inside China as the Communist element in the Kuomintang broke away from Chiang's rule and retreated to the North, to establish a Sovietized Marxist state.

Chiang, a Japanese-educated Army officer, was sent to Moscow by Sun Yat-sen for special training. Following Sun's death, the Generalissimo was "groomed" by the Russians to lead China. When he ultimately split with both the followers of Dr. Sun Yat-sen and with the Chinese Communists led by Mao Tse-tung, the civil war began.

Later, when the Japanese again invaded China, the Kuomintang Government and the Communists, instead of directing all their energies against the invaders, continued to fight each other. Not until 1937 did the Communist leader and Chiang Kai-shek make a fragile peace. By then Japan's entrance on the world scene and her alignment with Hitler's Germany and Mussolini's Italy were already leading Asia into World War II.

Ho Chi Minh of Vietnam, whose real name is Nguyen Ai Quoc, was born to an aristocratic Annamese family. He studied in France, after having first gone there during World War I to interpret for the corps of Chinese laborers employed in Europe.

A frail intellectual, Ho was a linguist who spoke excellent English and French, with a considerable knowledge of Russian, Chinese, and German. When the French Communist Party met in Tours, France, in 1920, Ho attended the meeting and became

Mao Tse-tung (left foreground) greets North Vietnam's Ho Chi Minh on his arrival in Peking for an official visit.—Wide World

a confirmed Marxist. He brought back his ideas of "liberation" to colonial Indochina and began the long road of revolution there.

During World War II Indochina was occupied by the Japanese, who had conquered the French there. When Japan's forces were in turn defeated by the victorious Allies, the French sought to return. But strong Indochinese nationalists formed effective resistance groups, led by Ho Chi Minh, and the return of French colonial rule was vigorously opposed. The Indochinese peninsula was then divided into three separate states—Vietnam, Laos, and Cambodia. Vietnam, with a 2,000-mile coastline, some 127,000 square miles of land and waterways, and a population of 30 million, was the largest state.

Still peace did not come. Protracted fighting broke out. In 1946, Ho Chi Minh's undisputed ability and personal prestige gained him the leadership of the Viet Minh—the dominant Vietnamese political resistance group—and peace efforts were begun.

In the agreement France, the dying colonial power, signed with Ho Chi Minh in 1946, *all* of Vietnam was recognized and was to take its place as a member of the Indochina Federation (with Laos and Cambodia) within the French Union. France was to aid the Vietnamese in ridding the state of the Chinese troops then in the country. Instead, diehard French colonists moved in troops and supplies and began a tragic extermination of Vietnamese nationalists. This coup d'état, reports Edgar Snow in his book *The Other side of the River,* was begun in May in Saigon, where the French set up a separate South Vietnam state as Ho Chi Minh and the Vietnamese delegation traveled to Paris to negotiate terms for the national elections and treaty accords of membership in the French Union.

Finally a treaty granting South Vietnam independence within the French Union was signed in December, 1949. The northern portion of the country, where bitter jungle warfare continued, was held by Ho Chi Minh and not included in the treaty agreement. Then, in 1950, both Britain and the United States recognized South Vietnam. North Vietnam was recognized by China and Russia. Asia's balance of power had shifted decisively. There was bound to be an effort by expansion-minded Communists to undermine the containment policy. It came soon—in Korea.

Chapter Ten

THE KOREAN WAR

> *"An immediate confrontation of the great powers."*
> —Former U.S. Assistant Secretary of State Harlan Cleveland

On the night of June 25, 1950, it is doubtful if one American in 10,000 knew the story of the 38th parallel. Among the far-flung corners of the globe where lonely and bored United States Army troops were on occupation duty was the one-time "Hermit Kingdom" of Korea. Europe had gotten most of the headlines. News about Asia mostly covered the Chinese struggle. The founding of NATO, the Berlin blockade, the airlift, and other European events held most people's attention.

But, as George Kennan said, "the towers of the Kremlin cast a long shadow." Just exactly how long was shown in the pitch-dark pre-dawn of June 25. Without warning, without any declaration of war, the well-trained army of the North Korean republic, equipped with the latest Russian weapons and T-34 tanks, rumbled across the 38th parallel and began a systematic slaughter of the South Korean Army and people.

The whine of Russian airplanes dive-bombing and the thunder of Russian heavy guns shattered the sense of relief the world had felt when the Berlin blockade was called off.

"How did it happen?" "What on earth *is* the Democratic People's Republic of Korea?" "What do we do now?" These were the bewildered questions Americans asked themselves when the first headlines broke. They learned that United Nations Secretary-General Trygve Lie had called an emergency meeting of the Security Council in New York for two o'clock that afternoon.

Commentators and news analysts began to sketch in the story. The war in Korea had its roots—as did so many other things—in the turmoil left over from the second World War. Japan had annexed Korea in 1905, following the war between Russia and Japan. For forty long years, until 1945, the Japanese had run Korea, filling the civic offices and operating what transportation there was. Korea has mountains running down its center which have been described as physically resembling a dinosaur's backbone. These almost impenetrable mountains make transportation from the east, bordered by the Sea of Japan, to the west, bordered by the Yellow Sea, virtually impossible.

When the Japanese were defeated in 1945 and sent back to their homeland, almost all of the doctors, engineers, civil officials, and other key people who had made things "go" in Korea also vanished. Mountainous, barren Korea struggled in chaos. American Army officers, trying to revive industry and transportation in South Korea, found themselves wrestling with heartbreaking problems. Due to Japanese repression, there were few skilled people to aid in Korea's recovery. Korea's extremes of climate—stifling heat in summer and bone-chilling cold in winter—and lack of good land for farming complicated the problem.

Why then was Korea important? Why, as history demonstrates, has the Korean peninsula, jutting out from Asia like a crooked thumb, so often been a battleground?

The answer is that Korea is a historic land bridge between Japan and rich Manchuria, which abounds in timber, iron, coal, and other resources. On the other hand, Korea is also a "dagger" from Manchuria aimed right at the heart of Japan. During hostilities, Korea's territory could be used by either Japan or Manchuria to menace the other.

As North Korean armored columns struck across the mountains, aiming at the southern capital of Seoul, the world had another example of how quickly decisions made at the end of the second World War had a way of "freezing" and hardening—because of the Cold War—into permanence.

The Potsdam Declaration proclaimed that Korea should be free and independent. Almost as an afterthought, a later American suggestion was accepted—that the Soviet Union should accept the Japanese surrender *north* of the 38th parallel, and the United States should accept the surrender *south* of that line. Then something that nobody had really anticipated took place. Korea was divided into two almost "airtight" occupation zones.

It was an arrangement that crippled an already poor country. Most of the mines and factories were in the north, while most of the farmland on which Korea's food was grown was in the south. Each half was really incomplete without the other.

The Soviet Union promptly closed its border north of the 38th parallel to all traffic. Not only did Soviet military commanders flatly refuse to work with American military commanders in solving Korea's problems, but the Soviets even refused to let Koreans who lived in the south visit relatives in the north. The "Bamboo Curtain" in Korea became an extension of the Iron Curtain in Europe.

For five years after the end of the second World War, Korea remained a backwater. The United States, hoping to prod the Soviet Union into some form of cooperation, brought the Korean question to the United Nations. A commission was set up, but the Soviet Union refused to even let the United Nations representatives into its zone! Frustrated, the United Nations restricted its operations to South Korea, where an election was organized under United Nations auspices. On May 10, 1948, Syngman Rhee, white-haired and autocratic, but pro-Western, was elected president.

The border between north and south remained sealed but far from quiet. Bloody hit-and-run raids by the North Koreans and fierce propaganda broadcasts from Pyongyang, promising "liberation" to the "oppressed peoples of the South," kept both North and South Korea in uneasy turmoil. The Soviet Union responded to the elections in South Korea by setting up the Democratic People's Republic of Korea with Kim Il Sung as Premier. Sung vowed to bring the "blessing" of Communism to *all* of Korea, south as well as north. The iron-willed Dr. Rhee matched Sung's vehemence in his vow that all Korea would be united under the south. The battle of words went on, punctuated by frequent raids over the 38th parallel.

Then, suddenly, for nearly three months (until June 25, 1950), the border was strangely quiet. The silence was ominous. What were the Communists up to? The ferocious artillery bombardment of June 25th, followed by the rumble of Russian T-34 tanks and invading armies, gave the answer.

The carefully planned sneak attack was, from the Communist

viewpoint, a smashing success. Many units of the South Korean (ROK) forces fought heroically, but they had no weapons to match the Russian heavy self-propelled guns and T-34 tanks. Rapidly, the Communist military machine ground South Korean divisions to pieces.

When word of the attack reached Washington, it was about 8:45 on a Saturday evening. First Secretary Wyo Wook Han of the Korean Embassy, better known in the capital as "Phil" Han, was getting ready to go to a party when he received an excited call from a friend in the Washington Bureau of the United Press. Han at once called Ambassador John Chang and informed him of the attack. The duty officer of the State Department was informed, and an emergency call went out at once to the Assistant Secretary of State for Far Eastern Affairs—a man who would later play an important role in the Cold War. His name was Dean Rusk. Rusk, in his dinner jacket, rushed to the State Department. After a conference, Rusk's recommendation was a fateful one—that the United States Army intervene in Korea to prevent a Communist triumph. President Truman was spending the weekend at his home in Independence, Missouri, when informed of the Communist attack. He immediately called a meeting of his top defense and diplomatic advisers for later that evening and then boarded his private airplane, *The Sacred Cow,* for the return to the capital. The decision of top American officials was virtually unanimous. The Soviet Union's puppet North Koreans must not be permitted to conquer South Korea.

By the time the United Nations Security Council met in New York at two o'clock on Sunday afternoon, with anxious diplomats clustered around its huge semicircular desk, the world was holding its breath. Could the United Nations do something effective to stop the aggression? If it couldn't—if the United Nations' member nations would not support it—it was finished. It might go on as a debating society, as the old League of Nations had done. But as a vital force in the world, it would be finished. No small nation would dare to trust its future to United Nations protection.

The session was tense with drama, and it was the occasion of a serious Russian diplomatic mistake. The chair of Soviet Delegate Andrei Gromyko was vacant. In the phrase of the day,

Gromyko and the other Soviet delegates had "taken a walk," dramatically boycotting the United Nations session over the seating of the Chinese Nationalist representative.

Events were later to prove that Gromyko's absence was a first-class blunder from the Russian viewpoint. Unhampered by the Soviet veto, the United Nations Security Council, at the urging of American Ambassador Warren Austin (a former United States Senator from Maine), passed a resolution calling for an immediate cease-fire in Korea and the withdrawal of North Korean troops behind the 38th parallel. All members of the United Nations were called upon to render every assistance to South Korea.

It is one thing to pass resolutions. It turned out to be quite another to stop the North Koreans' powerful military machine. Seoul, the capital of South Korea, was in confusion. American wives and children were evacuated by ship to Japan. The South Korean armies and United States residual forces were rapidly being overrun. Within three days, by June 28, Seoul had fallen. The Communists simply ignored the United Nations order to quit fighting.

President Truman ordered the United States Army, Navy, and Air Force to give every possible aid to South Korea and named General Douglas MacArthur, then heading the Military Occupation in Japan, as Commander of the United States forces.

American air power immediately entered the fight. The Far Eastern Air Force bombed North Korean airfields and began shooting Russian YAK fighters out of the skies. But the North Korean ground forces continued their advance. Air power alone was too little. The North Koreans would have to be defeated, if they could be defeated at all, by troops on the ground. General MacArthur flew from Japan to Seoul, viewed the streams of refugees and the disorganization of the South Korean troops, and advised Wahington that ground troops would be needed.

Hourly, the tension increased. Would Korea prove to be the beginning of the Third World War? Would Russia enter the war? Step by step, the Korean war escalated. An American combat team, and then two more divisions, were committed to Korea. The American Government, while determined to hold Korea, also tried hard to dampen the "war fever." Korea, the White House announced, was only "a police action." Later, the term "police action" and the manner in which the United States entered the Korean War—not by Act of Congress as the Constitution provided but in response to a challenge that had to be met immediately—would arouse great controversy. Nobody foresaw the course the Korean War would take. Both sides expected it would be over quickly. The grim truth was that the United States alone possessed the power to halt the North Korean invasion. Korea was a disturbing omen of things to come—the brush-fire wars that could erupt in far corners of the globe, small wars in which Americans would be sent to fight and die far from home. Like the later war in Vietnam, Americans were quickly to become deeply divided about Korea.

Thus began the concept of the "limited war"—something new to the United States. The limited war is fought for two aims: (1) to stop or contain Communist advance, and (2) to avoid the holocaust of a nuclear war. Could it be done? No man knew.

The first American efforts in Korea were marked by heroism—and defeat. The United States Army in Japan had been cut down to a skeleton five years after V-J Day. Units were understrength, weapons were old (mostly of World War II vintage), and ammunition was short. Troops were raw, not well trained, and far from combat-ready. Nobody expected a war. Or most thought that if there *were* a war, it would be fought by nuclear weapons, not by combat troops.

Now, a new realization slowly came. If the United States were to maintain peace—short of blowing up the whole world—it had to be ready with not only a nuclear arsenal, but also with the guns, rockets, tanks, and other equipment with which conventional armies fight. It was a grim realization, for it meant that twice as costly a defense establishment was needed.

Slowly, the American, United Nations, and Republic of Korea forces were forced back. Individual heroism by Americans such as the men of "Task Force Smith"—400 officers and men thrown hastily into the battle under the command of Charles B. Smith—failed to halt the advance and the group was routed in disorder. Riflemen and machine gunners could not stop tanks. Raw American troops could not stop the numerically superior, better-disciplined, better-equipped foe. More and more American troops from Japan were committed to the fight. All through July and August, until mid-September, the American and United Nations forces took a fearful beating. Dysentery, disease, and the searing heat, as well as the relentless enemy, took a terrible toll. By July 20, the North Koreans had pushed halfway through South Korea to capture Taejon. General William H. Dean, the American commander, was the last man to leave Taejon, but by that time the roads were blocked and he could not reach his retreating troops. General Dean made for the hills and mountains, eluding capture for thirty-five days before he was caught and made a prisoner of war. It was gallant heroism in the face of fearful odds. In defeat, however, he and his troops had bought precious time.

The retreat continued. By August, 1950, the United States and other troops fighting under the United Nations flag had been backed into a desperately small corner—the Pusan Perimeter—behind the Naktong River. The river, the rugged mountain range, and the Sea of Japan hemmed in the United Nations forces as the Communists launched a furious attack to gain control of all South Korea.

But the tide turned as more reserves were called in and General MacArthur issued what some have called a "fight or die" order, declaring that there would be no evacuation from Korea. Bit by bit, the shattered and demoralized Republic of Korea (ROK) and American armies were re-formed and reinforced with new equipment and manpower. American air and sea power continued to pound away at the Communists where their supply lines were already badly stretched and began to take a toll of Red ammunition.

It was a close thing, but the Pusan Perimeter was held.

On September 15, General MacArthur masterminded a campaign distinguished for its daring and brilliance. United States Marines electrified the free world by an amphibious landing from the sea at Inchon—18 miles from Seoul, the captured capital of South Korea—a risky, daring move. The tides at Inchon rise and fall more than 30 feet, and the channel leading to Inchon is narrow and surrounded by enormous mud flats. This allowed only a few hours a day for the invasion. Also high

United Nations troops land at Inchon, Korea, on September 15, 1950.—Wide World

sea walls would have to be scaled by the Marines—probably in the face of intense fire from the entrenched enemy.

Nevertheless, MacArthur insisted that the Inchon invasion was possible, and so it was. A huge amphibious task force of 70,000 men, headed by the Marines, overwhelmed the defenders and kept on going inland straight toward Seoul.

Now the rapid North Korean advance southward proved not a help but a disastrous hindrance to the invaders. The American, United Nations, and South Korean forces smashed through desperate Communist defenses to recapture Seoul—exactly three months to the day after the Communist attack across the 38th parallel. The bulk of the North Korean Army was then caught in a trap between United Nations forces above them at Seoul and below them at Pusan. MacArthur's forces cut their overextended supply lines to North Korea. The classic military "hammer-and-anvil" strategy could now be carried out, with the North Koreans caught between two armies and cut off from supplies and ammunition.

In the south, United Nations forces counter-attacked fiercely and broke out of the Pusan Perimeter. The North Koreans fought stubbornly at first; then their retreat became a flight. American air power, which had harassed the enemy's advance, now bombed and strafed the retreating soldiers. In a short, fierce campaign, the North Korean Army was destroyed. The Korean War seemed over.

In late September, 1950, the United States faced a momentous decision in Korea. The North Korean Army had been destroyed as an invading force, and the aggressors had paid a terrible price for their treachery. But what next? Should the armies halt at the 38th parallel or should North Korea be invaded and, if possible, re-united with South Korea under Syngman Rhee?

A demand for the surrender of North Korea went unanswered.

With hardly a pause, the United Nations forces swept north of the 38th parallel. Then the Red Chinese began to issue a series of warnings. On October 1, Chairman Mao Tse-tung declared in Peking: "The Chinese people . . . will not stand aside if the imperialists wantonly invade the territory of their neighbor." That became a favorite phrase of the Red Chinese.

Many studies were made of Red Chinese intentions. The decision was that the Chinese Communists were bluffing. The American-United Nations-ROK armies rolled through North Korea, more hindered by the mountains, rough terrain, and bad roads, than by the scattered North Korean opposition.

Some advance American troops reached the Yalu River—a place later to become well-known in the United States—the border between North Korea and Manchuria, a province of China.

The first sharp battles with the Chinese were fought late in October. Chinese forces, hidden in the vast ravines and valleys of North Korea, attacked and nearly destroyed a South Korean force. Then the enemy melted away again. Weeks passed.

Infiltrating silently, lying hidden by day and traveling by night, the Chinese Communists swarmed over the borders of North Korea. Avoiding roads, carrying their own supplies and ammunition, they laid a trap for the over-confident United Nations troops. They lay waiting for battle under their own conditions, minimizing the United Nations' air power and armor. In the wild terrain of North Korea, widely scattered United Nations units were hit hard and some almost annihilated. At the end of November, 1950, a series of ambushes wrecked terrible destruction upon the United Nations troops, who suddenly discovered that now *they* were the ones caught between the hammer and the anvil. Fighting through roadblocks and ambushes, amid fearful slaughter, the Americans soon realized they had a new war on their hands. This one was with the Communist Chinese.

Amid heroism and great losses, the United Nations forces retreated from North to South Korea. In one notable action, United States Army and Marines fought through to Hungnam, North Korea, and were evacuated by ship. Newspapers were filled with stories about the "Chinese hordes" that had burst across the border. There was much gloom among the United Nations forces in Korea; in the United States; everywhere in the free world. The Korean War had been escalated, enlarged. Would it escalate to the use of nuclear weapons?

The fighting in Korea's icy winter grew macabre. New United Nations lines were formed above Seoul, but "human waves" of Chinese peasants charged, overwhelmed the defenders, and threw them back. Then the United Nations armies would again rally. Indecisive, seesaw fighting raged up and down the peninsula.

Disagreement between General MacArthur and President Truman over Korean War strategy flared into the open. MacArthur wanted to bomb Red China, to set up a naval blockade of the Chinese coast, and to use Nationalist Chinese troops from Taiwan in the conflict. President Truman and his advisers were in total disagreement with this. Their aim was to dampen and to limit the Korean War; to try to "defuse" it, so that the Soviet Union would not openly enter the conflict. MacArthur protested the orders given him not to permit bombers to cross the Yalu River. Other members of the United Nations grew panicky at the very thought of an attack on Red China with its 700 million people. General Omar Bradley, Chairman of the United States Joint Chiefs of Staff—the heads of the Army, Navy, and Air Force—declared that a war with China would be "the wrong war, in the wrong place, at the wrong time."

Still the idea of a limited war was something entirely new to millions of Americans. "When you're in a war, you fight it to win it!" was a view constantly expressed. The climax of the Truman-MacArthur clash was reached when the five-star General wrote a letter to Congressman Joseph W. Martin of Massachusetts, ending with the ringing words: "There is no substitute for victory."

President Truman and his advisers decided they were having a difficult enough time explaining the Korean War to the American people and America's many allies anyway—without engaging in a running debate with the Commander over its purposes. President Truman removed MacArthur, undoubtedly one of the most brilliant generals in the annals of American military history, and named General Matthew Ridgway to succeed him.

The result was sensational. To millions and millions of Americans, MacArthur was a popular hero. The Korean War, fought without bugles and fanfare, was unpopular. When MacArthur returned to the United States, huge crowds and vast parades honored him everywhere. He was invited to address a Joint Session of Congress. MacArthur's eloquence, carried by television to a large audience, made him a martyr to all those who had no patience with the new, limited-war concept. But an emotional line in MacArthur's speech: "Old soldiers never die, they just fade away," proved prophetic. The controversy gradually faded away while many of Americans remained unconvinced of the correctness of the limited-war strategy. "War without victory"—a war to hold the line—was something entirely new in American thinking, and it became the policy of the Korean War.

In Korea, terrible devastation was being wrought upon helpless civilians caught between the armies. South Korea would later estimate its killed, wounded, and missing at 1,400,000 people. Among the United Nations troops fighting the Chinese and North Koreans were those of the United States, the United Kingdom, Canada, Turkey, Australia, Thailand, the Philippines, France, Greece, New Zealand, the Netherlands, Colombia, Belgium, Ethiopia, South Africa, and Luxembourg. The Red Chinese had more manpower but the United Nations forces had better guns and supplies, and most important, control of the air and sea.

On February 1, 1951, the United Nations General Assembly branded the Red Chinese as aggressors and called upon the

Central People's Government to withdraw from Korea. All United Nations members were called upon to resist aggression in Korea and to refrain from aiding in the aggression. Meanwhile, peace feelers went out.

From February until June, unending attempts were made to get the Communists to negotiate a peace to end the Korean War. The United States-United Nations forces disclaimed any intent to conquer North Korea. United States Secretary of State Dean Acheson, testifying before the Senate Foreign Relations Committee, said that a stable peace along the 38th parallel would be satisfactory.

The Communists were a long, long time deciding that they could not win a victory on the battlefield. Then on June 23, 1951, Soviet Delegate Yakov Malik made a speech in the United Nations indicating that a cease-fire was possible on the basis of mutual withdrawal behind the 38th parallel.

But a new complication entered the picture. President Syngman Rhee and the South Koreans, whose land had been devastated, were in no mood to accept a cease-fire. The Chinese offensive had been blunted, and the South Koreans scented victory. The offer of North Korean Premier Kim Il Sung, agreeing to a meeting at Kaesong, was accepted over Rhee's violent protests.

On July 1, 1951, an agreement to talk peace was reached. Many Americans and Westerners thought the Korean War was as good as over. More bitter lessons were to be learned, however. Nearly two years of protracted haggling and many bloody battles were to take place before peace returned to Korea.

Chapter Eleven

NATO STEMS
THE COMMUNIST TIDE
IN EUROPE

"A cornerstone of the security policy of its members"
　　—David H. Pepper, Director, Office of Atlantic Political and Military Affairs

On April 4, 1949, in the State Department Auditorium in Washington, D. C., a new chapter in the history of Western man was begun.

Flanked by banks of flowers and the brilliant hues of twelve national flags, twelve diplomats representing the leading Western European governments, Canada, and the United States, solemnly placed their signatures on the North Atlantic Treaty, binding their countries to a pact of common defense.

As Secretary of State Dean Acheson placed his signature on the historic document, America ended a century and a half of isolation from alliances with Europe. Only once before, during the American Revolution, had America joined with a foreign power in an alliance for mutual defense. Then the struggling colonies' representatives, acting under the Articles of Confederation, had signed a treaty with France in exchange for military and financial assistance in America's war with England.

Signing the North Atlantic Treaty pledged the United States to common defense with eleven other nations. It marked a historic turning-point in America's relations with the rest of the world. Ever since President George Washington's Farewell Address in 1796, reinforced by President Thomas Jefferson's warning to America to avoid "entangling alliances" in his Inaugural

Secretary of State Dean Acheson signs the NATO treaty on April 4, 1949.—U.S. Department of State

Address of 1801, the United States had shunned permanent alliances with other nations.

The North Atlantic Treaty was a measure of how much the Cold War had changed American thinking. The United States Senate, which must approve all treaties by a two-thirds majority, promptly ratified the North Atlantic Treaty. It was also signed by Belgium, Denmark, France, Iceland, Italy, Luxembourg, the Netherlands, Norway, Portugal, Great Britain, and Canada. Later, Greece, Turkey, and the Federal Republic of Germany (West Germany) would also join.

Now the Western nations had a treaty linking them together. It represented a startling new response to the challenge of the Cold War.

It was one thing to sign a treaty and quite different, and more difficult, to make NATO effective. To create an army and an organization for common defense and to encourage closer trade and cultural relations constituted a huge task. There were many serious problems to overcome; one of the most knotty was finding a way to allay France's traditional fear of Germany in order to gain French consent to the rearming of West Germany. How could this be done? More than a year and a half would pass before the answer was found.

Meanwhile, to what did the North Atlantic Treaty commit the United States? Here are the main points of the historic pact:

The peaceful settlement of disputes and abstinence from force or the threat of force. (Article 1)

The strengthening of economic ties among the signatory countries. (Article 2)

The strengthening of the means for resisting aggression, both by individual national efforts and by mutual assistance. (Article 3)

Consultation in the event of any signatory being threatened. (Article 4)

Mutual assistance in case of aggression. (This major provision is contained in Article 5, and express reference is made to Article 51 of the Charter of the United Nations, which recognizes the right of individual or collective self-defense.)

The establishment of a council charged with questions relative to the implementation of the Treaty relates to Article 9.

The signing of the North Atlantic Treaty for a time actually *increased* the danger of Soviet invasion rather than reducing it. There were rumors that the Soviets might strike fast in Western Europe before NATO had a chance to get organized. A defensive NATO army had to be created—and quickly. But the French kept "dragging their feet," as newspaper correspondents complained.

Secretary of State Acheson, whose well-tailored appearance led him to be described (in a hostile magazine article) as the "perfect diplomat, at least in appearance," played a key role in building NATO from a mere treaty into a force capable of stemming the Russian tide in Europe. Mr. Acheson, discussing his role with the authors, described those dangerous days: "The summer of 1950 was the most critical period in American foreign policy formulation in the postwar era." Several things, Secretary Acheson said, were important. The Berlin blockade had badly frightened Europe. The French political situation was critical—Premier Robert Schumann, for example, had just barely succeeded in throwing the Communists out—and the Marshall Plan was simply not going forward fast enough. More, much more, was needed, Mr. Acheson said.

With the Communist attack upon South Korea on June 25, 1950, a new shock wave struck the free world, arousing a greater awareness of the threats that confronted freedom worldwide. "The North Korean invasion was a striking demonstration that the Russians were prepared to use satellite force to gain their aims," Acheson said.

The Communist military victory in China had, of course, been a shattering blow to the balance of power in Asia. With the signing of the Sino-Soviet Alliance, which Premier Mao declared was a "thirty year treaty of friendship," the NATO Council, under its first chairman, Dean Acheson, centered its discussions on a single problem: how to defend the NATO area against an aggression similar to the one that had taken place in the Far East.

The NATO Council agreed that a "forward strategy" must be adopted. Any aggression had to be met and resisted, as far east as possible in Europe. It soon became apparent that far greater resources would be required than those then available—only fourteen Allied divisions were on the continent of Europe, against an estimated 200 Soviet divisions! Western military strength, NATO decided, would have to be greatly increased. It was also decided that the new "integrated NATO force" would have to be under "a centralized command, adequate to deter aggression and to ensure the defense of Western Europe."

This meant that the defense of Europe would have to begin on German soil and that NATO would have to include both the military and political participation of the Federal Republic of Germany. Secretary Acheson argued persuasively for this plan—with precise limitations and guarantees against any future German aggression of the kind that had earlier ravaged Europe.

Acheson, as an assistant secretary of state from 1941 to 1945, had worked closely with Secretary of State Cordell Hull, who had vigorously attacked the so-called "Morgenthau Plan" to turn postwar Germany into a strictly agrarian state. State Department officials feared that a reduced Germany, with no means to defend itself against future Communist expansion, would create a "power vacuum" in Central Europe into which Soviet power would necessarily flow. In 1950, Acheson believed that a strong and armed West Germany was necessary for creating any stable peace for Europe.

Nothing came of this proposal for many months. Much of Western European thought was still deeply rooted in distrust of either a unified or a strong Germany. An armed Germany seemed like madness to some. The French were particularly adamant in their stand against it. Finally an acceptable solution was agreed upon—the incorporation of West German armed forces into NATO, where they would be under international control. The French National Assembly and Government approved, and the proposal was submitted to the NATO Defense Committee on October 28, 1950.

The council deputies and the Military Committee readied a plan stipulating that "an acceptable and realistic defense of Western Europe and the adoption of a forward strategy could not be contemplated without active and willing German participation." It agreed that "participation must be within the NATO structure." Later, at the Brussels Conference of December 18, 1950, the Acheson cause won support. "German participation would strengthen the defense of Europe without altering in any way the purely defensive character of the North Atlantic Treaty Organization," he said, and the council ministers agreed.

Acheson then proposed that General Dwight D. Eisenhower, former Supreme Allied Commander in Europe, be named NATO's Supreme Allied Commander, Europe (SACEUR).

General Eisenhower came out of military retirement to undertake the massive task of building a NATO army from the many nations of Western Europe to counter the Soviet threat. For the first time ever in peacetime, a unified military command was created by the many jealous nations of Western Europe. The force also included soldiers from the United States and Canada, on the other side of the Atlantic.

Secretary of State Acheson was then under bitter attack in the United States, based on charges by Senator Joseph McCarthy of Wisconsin that he was "soft on Communism" and that the State Department was "riddled with Communists."

Upon Acheson's return from Brussels, President Truman sought to silence the critics:

> Mr. Acheson has helped shape and carry out policy of resistance to Communist imperialism. From the time of our sharing of arms with Greece and Turkey nearly four years ago, and coming down to the recent moment when he advised me to resist the Communist invasion of South Korea, no official in our government has been more alive to Communism's threat to freedom or more successful in resisting it.

From its beginnings, the North Atlantic Treaty Organization was one of the marked Western successes of the Cold War. Great credit for effective work in the face of difficulty belongs to former Secretary of State Acheson, much-abused in the McCarthy era. Acheson is important for another reason, too—for bringing the professional diplomat to the fore in the vital role of American Secretary of State. Too often in the past, the secretary of state, whose post is second only to the presidency in its complex and difficult problems, has been a political appointee. The Cold War brought a realization of how important to American security are the secretary of state and America's ambassadors. It is unlikely that presidents will ever go back to making such appointments to pay off their political debts.

Acheson was born in Middletown, Connecticut, the son of an Episcopal bishop. He made a brilliant record at Yale and Harvard, served as undersecretary of the Treasury, resigned to practice law, and served as assistant secretary and under secretary of State before becoming secretary.

Assistant Secretary of State for European Affairs John M. Leddy said:

> Looking back at NATO since the signature of the North Atlantic Treaty in 1949, one is struck by the fact that it has been an outstanding success. It has fulfilled, and it continues to fulfill, its central purpose of keeping the peace and creating a climate of security . . . it has not only survived but has evolved, mostly by small steps indiscernible to the public eye, into something much more than a purely military organization designed to provide an integrated military defense of the North Atlantic Treaty area against the contingency of war.

Leddy added that it is this political evolution of NATO that promises to become the dominant characteristic of the NATO of the future, despite France's withdrawal from participation in the integrated NATO military system. It must be remembered that at the French "defection," the remaining fourteen allies promptly issued a joint statement reaffirming their determination to continue and to make whatever adjustments were needed to defend the NATO area without France if that should become necessary, providing the viability of the structure itself.

March 19, 1951, saw another major step in the protection and recovery of Western Europe—the drafting of a fifty-year treaty setting up a coal and steel pool among six nations—West Germany, France, Italy, Belgium, the Netherlands, and Luxembourg. This working together by eliminating tariff barriers and pooling the basic productive sinews of industry was to lead to the founding of the European Common Market, another important step in eliminating old rivalries and hatreds and increasing production.

On May 2, 1951, West Germany was admitted as a full member of the Council of Europe. With Marshall Plan help, with the receding of the Soviet threat because of NATO, and the freeing of trade and business from artificial barriers built around nations, the long-delayed recovery of Western Europe began to rush ahead.

On April 28, 1952, another vastly important step was taken to wipe out the last remnants of the second World War. A peace treaty with Japan, negotiated in spite of the vigorous efforts of the Soviets to block it, became effective. Japan also signed a mutual assistance treaty with the United States. Its important weight was added to that of the free world in the Pacific—a badly needed weight, for the Communists, thwarted in Europe, were again plotting new trouble in Asia.

Chapter Twelve

PEACE IN KOREA
AND WAR IN VIETNAM

"The United States is no less a Pacific than an Atlantic power."
—United States Under Secretary of State, Eugene V. Rostaw

In the late summer of 1952, the political situation in the United States dramatically changed. President Truman declined to run for re-election. The Democratic Party chose Adlai E. Stevenson, Governor of Illinois, to run for president. His Republican opponent was General of the Armies Dwight D. Eisenhower. From the first, the public opinion polls showed the enormously popular General Eisenhower far ahead. He was aided by the Republican campaign taunt: "Communism, Corruption, Korea."

Scandals in the Internal Revenue Service, the Reconstruction Finance Corporation, the Agriculture Department, and other government agencies during the Truman Administration hurt Stevenson badly. So did the administration's alleged "softness" toward Communism. Millions believed Senator Joseph McCarthy's charges that the State Department was "honeycombed with Communists." (In fairness, it should be noted that the Truman Administration, whatever its faults, will be remembered for its firm and effective steps to prevent the spread of Communism. Still, millions of Americans believed that the administration was "soft on Communism.")

Most of all, perhaps, Americans were tired of the bloody stalemate in Korea, which was costing 2,000 American dead and wounded per month. In October, 1952, General Eisenhower made a promise. If elected, he said, he would go to Korea personally and see what could be done about ending the conflict.

In November Eisenhower won by a landslide, capturing 442 electoral votes to Stevenson's 89.

The prolonged negotiations of the Korean truce were stalemated over the issue of forced "repatriation" of prisoners of war. Many captured North Korean and Chinese Communist soldiers did not want to return to their homelands. The Communists insisted that *all* prisoners of war, willing or unwilling, must return. Efforts to obtain a cease-fire were also complicated by Syngman Rhee's adamant "never." Rhee insisted that the United Nations forces fight on to victory.

Even as the negotiations in Korea dragged on while fighting still continued, new and bitter fighting broke out in Vietnam. Ho Chi Minh, capitalizing on the rising tide of sentiment for independence from European colonial status that was sweeping Asia and Africa, began the offensive that was to astonish the Western world. His Viet Minh followers, carrying weapons and ammunition on their backs through jungles, mountains, and swamps, faced the French in bloody fighting. At first, Americans paid little attention to the fighting, few dreaming that they would become involved. The peace treaty with Japan and a coup d'état in Egypt, in which the fat, corrupt King Farouk was ousted by a group of Army officers headed by Major General Mohammed Neguib, received far more attention in the American press. (A few farsighted correspondents wrote that an obscure colonel named Nasser seemed to be the real strong man in the group.)

Events drifted along uneasily. On November 15, 1952, the United States Atomic Energy Commission announced that the awesome atomic bomb had an even more awesome successor— the hydrogen bomb. The menace of mass destruction seemed more fearful than ever.

Then, on March 5, 1953, from within the grim, fortress-like walls of the Kremlin, came stunning news—

STALIN DEAD!

Newspapers of the world, even in the West, filled pages and pages with photographs and stories about the career of the man who had dominated Russia for so many years. Was Stalin murdered or did he die a natural death? Lurid stories, which have not yet been proved or disproved swept the world. Some whispered that Stalin had been poisoned or strangled when he had seemed likely to recover from a lingering illness. Certainly it is known that Stalin had planned another in his series of bloody purges. Many of his successors, who inherited part of his vast power, had had good reason to wish him dead. The truth about Stalin's death may never be known. In his lifetime, Stalin had led the Soviet Union's development from a backward nation to a superpower and more. The Kremlin's tentacles reached into Communist parties in every nation in the world.

Now the important question was, would the Cold War change? Stalin, more than any other man, was its architect. Who would take power in Russia? What would happen?

In the Soviet Union, Stalin had been built up by propaganda into an almost godlike figure. Tens and hundreds of millions publicly mourned him in elaborate funeral ceremonies. He was solemnly installed beside Lenin in the mausoleum that is almost a religious shrine to the Russian people. In the United States Secretary of State John Foster Dulles despatched a cold message: "The Government of the United States tenders its official condolences to the Union of Soviet Socialist Republics on the death of Generalissimo Josef Stalin, Prime Minister of the Soviet Union." There was not a single word of praise for the deceased Russian dictator from the stiff-necked Secretary Dulles.

The question of the succession following Stalin's death was tentatively answered by the establishment of a triumvirate of three men. Georgi Malenkov, Stalin's pudgy, black-haired favorite, who was powerful in the party apparatus, became the new premier and secretary of the all-important Communist party. The two others were the sinister Lavrenti P. Beria, head of the secret police, and the icy-cold V. M. Molotov, Foreign Minister of the Soviet Union, best-known to the world at large.

It may be one of the tragedies of history that Malenkov did not last very long as premier of the Soviet Union and that his brief, less than two-year tenure saw his powers eroded to virtually nothing. Malenkov was stained with the blood of Stalin's purges, but he was highly intelligent and well educated. Malenkov was well aware of the ruin that could accompany a nuclear war. Almost his first act was to sound a hopeful note in a speech. The difficulties between the Soviet Union and the United States could be solved by peaceful means, Malenkov said.

But behind the scenes, a fierce struggle for power was taking place in the Kremlin. Malenkov seems to have overreached himself, striving for too much of Stalin's power, and to have alarmed his colleagues. On March 21, 1953, only sixteen days after Stalin's death, it was blandly announced that Malenkov had "voluntarily" given up his post as secretary of the Communist Party—the route that Stalin had used to gain power—and that the post was to be temporarily filled by his almost unknown rival, Nikita Khrushchev. From that day foreward, Malenkov's star was steadily to fall and Khrushchev's to rise.

The Soviet Union was obviously in turmoil. But Malenkov's words suggest that the U.S.S.R. was prepared to dampen down the Cold War. In London, Winston Churchill, back in power as Britain's prime minister, called for a new meeting of heads of governments to ease tensions.

Meanwhile, in the harsh world of Walter Ulbricht's East Germany, there began a dramatic series of events that may have helped to undermine Malenkov's attempted rapprochement with the West—the East German uprising. It was important not only in itself, but as a violent reminder to the Soviets of just how shaky was the empire the U.S.S.R. had seized with tanks and bayonets in Eastern and Central Europe.

Stalin's death, the removal of the iron fist, had shaken the Communist satellite countries of Europe—East Germany, Hungary, Rumania, Bulgaria, and all the rest felt the effects. In the temporary uncertainty, nobody knew what would happen.

But then, like a flash of lightning glaring over a murky swamp, on June 17, 1953, the world had a surprising demonstration of how the captive peoples of Europe felt about their Communist masters.

"Strike! Come and join the strike!" It all began simply enough as a strike by the workers of Block 40 on Stalinallee—East Berlin's Communist showcase street—for better pay and for relief from the inhuman "work norms" laid upon them. It had begun —revealingly—at a Communist-sponsored meeting to have the workers "approve" a state-imposed increase of 10 percent in the amount of work a worker had to do in order to earn full wages. But the carpenters, bricklayers, and construction workers of Block 40 had had enough of Communist slogans and meetings. They wanted their pay. Instead of meekly agreeing to the increase, as they had always done before, the workers rebelled. The 400 workers of Block 40 decided to parade down Stalinallee in a body.

As they passed, workers from other projects gasped in astonishment—and then joined the growing parade to the government headquarters. Past Marx-Engels Square, down the ruined, bomb-scarred Unter den Linden, the ever growing throng defiantly paraded. Onlookers joined. There were defiant shouts for Walter Ulbricht to come out and talk with them. Soon tens of thousands of East Germans were parading through the streets, shouting for free elections and demanding that Ulbricht resign. Soviet slogans and propaganda were torn down. In West Berlin, RIAS (Radio In American Sector) broadcast the news. Throughout East Germany rebellion broke out against the Communists. Jails were broken into and political prisoners freed. In Halle, the Communist SED Party headquarters were burned. In Rathenow, a police informer who had denounced hundreds of East Germans to the Communist secret police was beaten to death.

All over East Germany, Russian T-34 tanks appeared on the streets—a prelude to what was to happen in Hungary three years later. Courageous men and women fought the tanks with stones and their bare hands, but it was a one-sided contest. Communist firing squads were kept busy for several days, executing "criminals" who had taken part in the uprising. The Western Powers denounced the Soviet reprisals as "brutality that will shock the world."

In that one lightning flash, East Germans had shown that only the brute force of Soviet tanks and bayonets held them in bondage. It was a lesson that made the Communist masters of other Soviet satellites in Europe tremble.

During the single year of 1953, 331,390 East Germans, because of their desire for freedom and because of fear, arrests, and political purges, "voted with their feet" and escaped to the West.

On the front line of the continuing struggle of the Cold War, at Panmunjom, Korea at 10:01 in the morning of July 27, 1953, a treaty was finally signed between members of the free world and those of the Communist bloc. It had taken two years, seven-

East Berliners watch a Communist propaganda booth burn during the June riots in 1953.—United Press International

teen days, and 225 meetings, (first in a teahouse in Kaesong on North Korean territory and then in makeshift tents) to bring about the "settlement" and the uneasy peace. An estimated 18 million words had been exchanged in seemingly endless discussions before the agreements to end the stalemated Korean War came about and the negotiators were able to walk out of the final meeting hall. Not a friendly word or even a handshake passed between the delegates during the eleven-minute ceremony.

The agreement called for a political conference on unification and withdrawal of foreign troops; yet, fourteen years later, troops would still guard their respective sides of the North-South boundary—the *DMZ* that marches for 151 miles across the Korean peninsula.

Even the international conference in Geneva in 1954 failed to turn the Korean truce agreements into a real peace. By late 1953, in fact, a disastrous defeat suffered by French forces at the hands of Ho Chi Minh's Viet Minh had shifted the emphasis away from Korea to Southeast Asia.

With Indochina cut in two and the French losing ground daily, an invasion of Northern Laos by a division of the Communist Viet Minh took place. It led the United States to send military aid to the French forces. For on February 6, 1954, the United States Department of Defense announced it was sending B-26 light bombers to Indochina, with 105 Air Force technicians.

On February 18, 1954, the foreign ministers of France, the U.S., Great Britain and the Soviet Union had called for an international meeting to discuss both the situation in Korea and that in Indochina. Then on March 13, 1954, a massive assault was launched by the forces of Ho Chi Minh against the isolated outpost of French forces at Dien Bien Phu. In a few weeks the struggle was over. Dien Bien Phu fell on May 7.

On May 8, delegates to the Geneva Conference that had convened on April 26 began to gather to discuss peace for Southeast Asia. The participants were France, the State of Viet Nam, the Viet Minh (DRV), Laos, Cambodia, Communist China, the Soviet Union, Britain and the United States.

The cessation of hostilities agreement between France and the Viet Minh was signed on July 21, 1954—an agreement that did not include the voice of South Vietnam (the Viet Nam

State). This final declaration of the conference was approved by a voice vote of the participating nations with the exception of the South Viet Nam and United States representatives who protested the partitioning of Viet Nam.

The United States said that it would "refrain from the threat or use of force to disturb the final declaration," but that "in the case of nations now divided against their will, we shall continue to seek to achieve unity through free elections supervised by the United Nations to insure they are conducted fairly." The United States still holds this position today.

Secretary of State Dulles felt it necessary to clarify the United States policy and official position:

> The imposition on Southeast Asia of the political system of Communist Russia and its Chinese Communist ally, by whatever means, would be a grave threat to the whole free community. The United States feels that that possibility should not be passively accepted, but should be met by united action. This might involve serious risks. But these risks are far less than those that will face us a few years from now, if we dare not be resolute today.

Continuing pressure by the Communists in Vietnam, Laos, Cambodia, and the Formosa Straits and the drawing together of the Chinese Communists and Indonesia in intensified political exchanges and trade agreements led to a new step by the United States in this vast area of the world—the signing of the Southeast Asia Defense Organization (SEATO) Treaty, which was concluded at Manila on September 8, 1954. Parties to the agreement (which the Soviet Union furiously denounced as "a threat to security in Asia"), were the United States, Australia, France, New Zealand, Pakistan, the Philippines, Thailand, and the United Kingdom.

The pact, signed in the Philippines' hot, steamy capital of Manila, pledged the signatory nations "to meet the common danger."

The SEATO treaty was an extension of the Anzus security treaty that had been signed earlier by the United States, Australia, and New Zealand for self-help and mutual aid and to coordinate their efforts for "collective defense for the preservation of peace pending the development of a more comprehensive system of regional security in the Pacific area." SEATO was also an extension of the already successful progress of NATO in Europe.

SEATO was originally conceived as a non-exclusive organization, open to all the nations of Southeast Asia willing to share its benefits and its responsibilities. The treaty was not designed as an exclusively military document but provided in many of its articles for cooperation in economic, social, and cultural measures to promote economic progress and social well-being among the member nations.

The SEATO headquarters were set up at Bangkok, Thailand. Its treaty obligation area includes "the whole of South-East Asia and the South-West Pacific below 21 degrees 30 minutes north latitude and the entire territories of the Asian partners—Pakistan, the Philippines and Thailand."

The effects of the SEATO treaty are still being felt today.

The Korean War, though it brought victory to neither side, was a landmark in the Cold War. It made a major world power out of Communist China and gave it tremendous prestige in Asia. The Chinese Communists had fought the West to a standstill—a feat that made them, in the words of Secretary Dulles, "dizzy with success."

Henceforth, Asian Communists would be wary of what Secretary of State Dean Rusk would later describe as "Phase Two" of aggression—the marching of hostile enemies openly across national borders. ("Phase One," as described by Secretary Rusk, is a nuclear exchange, which is not a rational act unless one wants to blow up the world.) After Korea, Communist aggression would concentrate on "Phase Three," infiltration and subversion in secret.

The Korean War was intensely controversial in the United States. Was Korea a victory or was it a defeat? The idea of containing Communism had registered with few Americans. People wanted to talk in terms of victory and defeat as in all other wars.

Secretary Dulles cited arguments that Korea was a victory. "For the first time in history an international organization has stood against an aggressor and has marshalled force to meet force," Dulles told the American people in a statement of the United States position:

The aggressor, at first victorious, has been repulsed. The armistice leaves him in control of less territory than when his aggression began, and that territory is largely wasted.

The North Korean army is virtually extinct, the Chinese and Korean Communist armies have sustained about two million casualties, and of the ten million people of North Korea, one out of every three has died from the war ravages and the inhuman neglects which their rulers have imposed. These tragic results will surely be pondered by other potential nominees for aggression-by-satellite.

Politicians would continue to wrangle over whether Korea was a victory or a defeat. But, from the standpoint of the free world, the basic fact remained that, for the first time in history, an international organization—the United Nations—*had,* however laboriously, managed to get a score of nations to fight to preserve their collective security.

Chapter Thirteen

THE COLD WAR SPREADS TO THE MIDDLE EAST

> *"There can never, in the long run, be an honest and dependable peace unless there is justice and law."*
> —John Foster Dulles

War clouds darkened the horizon as 1955 began. Both the United States and the U.S.S.R. already possessed the awesome thermonuclear weapons. Both discovered that Communist China had arisen on the world scene, almost like the proverbial sleeping dragon. It was a bellicose, expansionist dragon at that.

Nationalist Chinese Formosa and the Pescadores were the threatened areas coveted by the Red Chinese. A violent "Hate America" campaign had begun in China. Typical Chinese Communist pamphlets read: "We must hate America. Because It Is A Corrupt Imperialist Nation, the World Center of Reaction and Decadence." "We Must Look Down Upon America Because She Is A Paper Tiger And Entirely Vulnerable To Defeat."

Boasts from Radio Peking that Communist China planned to conquer Formosa, where Chiang's government-in-exile was in residence, and to take the Pescadores and other offshore islands, created a full-scale crisis. Repeated artillery bombardment of the Pescadores led the Eisenhower Administration to ask Congress for what was described as a "blank check" to use American armed forces to prevent a Red Chinese invasion.

Secretary Dulles, after testifying before a joint meeting of the House of Representatives Foreign Affairs Committee and the Senate Foreign Relations Committee gained a 409-to-3 House vote and an 85-to-3 Senate vote in favor of strong action. His "brink of war" talks, backed up by Congressional approval of American armed intervention, led to the signing of a mutual defense pact with the Nationalist Chinese, which the Secretary felt would dramatically underscore United States intentions.

The United States would use force against force, Dulles declared. He warned Americans that the Chinese Communists "constitute an acute and imminent threat more likely to lead to war than the Russian threat."

During these trying days, United States officials and British Foreign Secretary Anthony Eden worked feverishly to prepare a compromise to settle the Formosa crisis. Though the shelling of the offshore islands continued, the Chinese Communists gradually began to talk less and less about an impending invasion of Formosa, and, little by little, the crisis began to recede.

In 1955, emphasis shifted again in the changing battlegrounds of the Cold War as hopeful signs of a detente between East and West began to appear. Stalin's death had already led to milder tones toward the West from the Soviet Union. By May 1955, an agreement on the evacuation and neutralization of Austria was finally reached and the Austrian peace treaty became a reality.

The American price for the calling of a summit conference that the Russians desired was an end to Soviet obstruction of the long delayed Austrian peace treaty—ten years after the close of World War II. The Soviets, anxious for the conference, agreed to return control of the Austrian oil fields to the Austrians and to turn back to them control of the Danube Steamship Company —two of the last stumbling blocks to the signing of peace. The treaty freed Austria after seventeen long years of occupation— first by the Nazis and then by the conquering Allies. The day of the signing found hundreds of thousands of Viennese parading through the streets of their freed capital. No longer would the city's four zones of occupation hear the sound of marching sentries.

In the treaty negotiations the United States urged the deletion of references to the war guilt of the Austrian people. Instead it insisted that the Austrians be treated as victims of Nazi aggression, that no reparations be demanded of her, and that the treaty be called a "state treaty" rather than a peace treaty. Russia, in turn, insisted that Austria remain a neutral nation. Under the terms of the treaty she was not allowed to align herself with the West or join the NATO ranks of the free world. Nor could she join the recently completed Warsaw Pact—concluded among the Soviet-bloc nations as a counteroffensive to NATO and the Marshall Plan.

The calling of the Summit Conference of the "Big Four" in July 1955 enhanced the hopes of the world that, perhaps, a change within the Soviet Union had taken place and solutions to mutual world problems would be eased. The Twentieth Communist Congress that was held the following year finally revealed to the world that great changes had been occurring within the Soviet Union. For it was at the Congress held in Moscow in midwinter 1956 that the large scale plans for "deStalinization" were announced.

The conferees at the Summit Conference were President Dwight D. Eisenhower of the U.S., Prime Minister Anthony Eden of Britain, Premier Edgar Faure of France and Premier Nikolai Bulganin of the U.S.S.R. Their aides were Dulles of the United States, Harold MacMillan of Britain, and Nikita Khrushchev of Russia. It was here that Russia's rising new star, Khrushchev, first came onto the world scene. "This is a new era, things are different," he proclaimed amid much handshaking and many broad smiles. But behind the facade Russian obstructionism continued. Disarm Germany and disband NATO or there would be no peace and no security, they maintained. Publicly, however, Russia at long last agreed to the reunification of Germany on the basis of free elections—or so the delegates and the press thought. These hopes were later dashed when the Russians refused to carry through the promises given at the conference.

One of the problems raised by the high hopes for the outcome of the summit conference was the fact that little actually was accomplished despite the fanfare. At the Foreign Ministers' Conference held later in the fall, it was understood that agreements reached at the midsummer conference would be translated into action. The only problem was that the ministers discovered that nobody had agreed on what had been agreed on in the first place! Soviet Foreign Minister Molotov and American Secretary of State Dulles were at almost immediate loggerheads on the agenda. Molotov officially presented a chilling program of action —America must withdraw from Europe and dismantle NATO. Then he repudiated Russia's earlier agreement for free elections in Germany. The ministers' meeting ended in recriminations and charges of bad faith on both sides.

Dulles wryly reported to the nation: "For the past few weeks, I've been negotiating with the Russians at Geneva, and that's quite a job. As I expect you know, this Geneva agreement didn't get us very far in negotiations and agreements. . . . In fact, it didn't get us anywhere at all."

1955 also saw the Cold War return to the Middle East—an arena from which Soviet pressures had been absent since the dramatic days following World War II. In 1955 an anti-Soviet alliance that was to be known as the Baghdad Pact was entered into by Iran, Turkey, and Iraq. It drew Soviet protests, but not until Britain became a signatory did any unforeseen Cold War adventures began. Britain's admittance in April led the nationalist Egyptians to regard the alliance as something of an anti-Egyptian as well as an anti-Soviet agreement. It led to the development of stronger and stronger ties between Egypt and Russia —ties that included heavy Communist-bloc aid that would eventually send strong Cold War currents and countercurrents drifting across the ancient land of the pharaohs.

To the American public, Egypt's techniques of "shopping around" for aid money in both the West and the Soviet Union created strong misgivings as to Nasser's objectives. But weighed against this objection to Nasser's free-wheeling neutrality was the country's immense strategic and political importance. Egypt had long been Europe's lifeline due to the location of the Suez Canal, and the shrewd and ambitious Colonel Nasser had succeeded in making Egypt the single most important and most influential nation in the entire Arab world.

Secretary of State Dulles had strong objections to Nasser's playing off American offers of aid against rumored bids from Russia of massive financial assistance in building a high dam at Aswan to make more arable land available in that parched and needy section of the world. In spite of his views, Dulles reluctantly asked Congress to authorize a long-term commitment of American dollars for the project.

The proposed financing of the Aswan Dam called for, among other things, a United States grant of $56 million, plus British aid in the amount of $14 million. Interestingly enough, it never appeared that the proposed funding would bring either the United States or Britain much good will for their money. Active anti-American and anti-British campaigns were going on in Egypt while the negotiations were taking place! At the same time, Nasser was seeking Russian aid for the project to be able to push the dam construction ahead more quickly than the successive stages originally called for. Meanwhile, rumors that Russia had already agreed to finance the entire billion-dollar construction at a very low interest rate—1 or 2 percent—scored heavy propaganda victories for the Communists in the Middle East.

By July, 1956, American public opinion and Dulles' exasperation led to a dramatic explosion over the Aswan Dam issue. In a surprise move Dulles abruptly withdrew America's offer of aid to Egypt. A vast shift of sentiment away from Nasser and Egyptian problems had taken place in the United States as Egypt's anti-American campaign grew in size and volume.

A week later, however, it was the Western world's turn to be stunned by a turn of events in far-off Egypt. Nasser, bitter at America's and Britain's withdrawals of aid, seized control of the Suez Canal, nationalizing it as Egyptian property on Egyptian soil. Nasser announced to the world that he would use the profits to build the Aswan Dam!

"He can't be allowed to get away with it," thundered one prominent London newspaper of Nasser's seizure of the Canal. This pretty well summed up the reactions of the West.

Nasser's action seemed clearly illegal. Egyptian police had simply marched into the offices of the Suez Canal Company and taken over. But Egypt was a party to the Treaty of 1888, under which the Suez Canal Company held a valid lease until 1968.

Both Britain and France talked of war. Secretary Dulles urged caution and got the two nations to agree to an international conference of canal-using nations, which was set for August 16. The eight nations that had signed the Treaty of 1888, plus sixteen other countries whose shipping was vitally affected by the Egyptian seizure of the Canal, were invited to the conference— Soviet Russia included. Egypt, however, declined to attend.

Egypt refused to abide by any of the proposals made at the London Conference that summer of 1956, and the Suez crisis dragged on. Nasser refused to negotiate. Britain and France, the nations most vitally affected, grew restive and began to talk of force. There was open talk of "shooting their way through" the Canal.

A second London Conference was called, and the United States put forward a plan for the formal organization of a Canal Users' Association that would assure permanent, dependable, and efficient operation, maintenance, and development of the Canal with scrupulous respect of Egyptian sovereignty.

For a short time, it looked as if a peaceful and satisfactory solution might be found. The United Nations Secretary-General, Dag Hammarskjöld, met informally with Egyptian representatives and those of Britain and France. A set of principles was tentatively agreed upon: 1) there should be no discrimination among canal-user nations, 2) the Canal should be kept free from politics (i.e. Cold War shifts and balances), and 3) Egypt's sovereignty would be respected.

On October 29, all was blown away. The news tickers of the world carried the ominous announcement that Israel had invaded Egypt! Israel was quickly joined by both France and Britain. There was a shooting war in the Middle East. America was not notified until it heard the news on the air.

The damage to the Western Alliance was staggering. "NATO has been dealt a death blow," solemnly declared Senator Walter F. George, Chairman of the Senate Foreign Relations Committee. Newspapers all over America savagely denounced this "betrayal" of America by France, Britain, and Israel. Some wrote: "Dulles has been caught napping," and called for his resignation. World opinion, which had been violently anti-Nasser, switched in his favor. The Russians spoke threateningly of sending "volunteers" to aid Egypt in the fighting.

In the United Nations, Secretary Dulles dramatically called for a cease-fire. His resolution passed, 64-to-5. The United States' old friends and allies—Britain, France, Israel, Australia, and New Zealand—voted "no." Finally, the fighting stopped. The split in the Atlantic Alliance was gradually healed, but with the result that the Cold War had spread again to the Middle East.

Events had moved quickly throughout the summer and fall of 1956. In early summer an abortive uprising occurred in Posnan,

Ships sunk in the Suez Canal at Port Said, Egypt, keep the canal from being used during the Suez Crisis in 1956.—United Press International

Poland. It led to the rise of Premier Wladyslaw Gomulka and much liberalization of Communist Poland's structure—but these were only reforms within the limits of a Sovietized society. Then, on October 24th, an ill-fated, tragic revolt against the Soviet Union and the Communist dictatorship's puppet government broke out in Hungary. Massive anti-Soviet riots occurred. On November 1 the newly installed nationalist Hungarian Premier, Imre Nagy, appealed to the United Nations for help. But Soviet tanks and army units poured into Hungary. The Hungarian people's short-lived bid for freedom from the Soviet orbit was smashed with fearsome brutality. Thousands of Hungarians were slain in bitter street fighting and reprisals taken in the aftermath of the abortive revolt by Hungarian citizens. On November 4, 1956, Moscow radio announced the formation of a new Hungarian government under Communist First Secretary Janos Kadar. On November 23, the Yugoslav press reported that Soviet security police had Premier Nagy in custody. He was later executed by the Communists.

The United Nations, in a futile post-mortem session late in December, denounced its Security Council member, the Soviet Union, in a censure move against Russia's intervention in the Hungarian revolt. The United States, too, was singled out for blame by many critics outside the halls of the United Nations. The United States had, many small nations believed, promised aid to revolutionists who wished to throw off the yoke of Communism. But when such an attempt had been made—as in Hungary, with huge grass-roots support—many charged that the United States had failed to keep its promise.

The new year, 1957, augured still more defeats for the West. In the Far East, affairs continued badly. In a surprise move, President Achmed Sukarno of Indonesia called on his country to abandon its government based on Western-style democracy to adopt a new style of government that would include cooperation with Indonesia's growing Communist Party. Sukarno declared a state of martial law while the changeover took place.

In Europe, the government of Premier Gomulka and his National Unity front won an overwhelming victory in the Polish parliamentary elections. The election gave the voters, for the first time in any Communist state, some freedom of choice. Later in the year, encouraged by the winds of change, the United States signed an agreement with Poland, giving her a $48.9 million loan for purchases of farm-surplus commodities and mining machinery. By May, 1957, America had even resumed military aid to Yugoslavia, which continued in its free-wheeling form of Communism, despite new and closer ties with the Soviet Union.

Soviet gains continued, too. Although a special United Nations committee made a sweeping indictment of the Soviet intervention in Hungary and the murdering of Hungarian citizens, the Middle East seemed to be drawing more and more into the Soviet camp. On July 23, 1957, Nasser's triumphant Egypt made an impressive display of a vast arsenal of Soviet-built military equipment and aircraft. The event was the fifth anniversary of the ouster of King Farouk's government. By late summer, the Soviet Union announced that it would send an economic mission to Syria to help in an extensive industrial and transportation program. The move was followed on August 13 by the Syrian Government's ousting of three United States Embassy officials who were accused of plotting to overthrow the Syrian Government. The United States retaliated by expelling the Syrian Ambassador from the United States.

Missile rattling shook the world's tranquillity for the first time. The Soviet Union established a missile base on Peter the Great Bay near Vladivostok and later announced the successful test of the world's first intercontinental multi-stage ballistic missiles. By October 4, the drama of the missile age was succeeded by the even more dramatic space age. The Soviet Union astounded the world with its announcement that it had launched the first man-made satellite into space. "Sputnik," the Russian word for satellite, became a household word around the globe. In November, Russia launched a second, larger Sputnik, and a shaggy white dog became the world's first living occupant of a spacecraft.

The United States, perhaps a little embarrassed, launched its first Atlas intercontinental ballistic missile in December, followed by an equally successful testing of the intermediate Jupiter ballistic missile.

The space race was on. With it came a new shift in Cold War techniques.

Chapter Fourteen

EUROPEAN RECOVERY, A BERLIN BOMBSHELL, AND CHAOS IN THE CONGO

"One fact must be faced squarely. Fear and appeasement will not in the long run reduce the danger of war. Only courage and a firm stand on our rights and principles can do this."
—United States Secretary of State Christian Herter

In the late 1950's and early 1960's headlines in the world's press were often dominated by a pudgy, squat, baldheaded little man who looked—and sometimes chose to play—the role of a hilarious, roly-poly clown. This was Nikita Sergeyevich Khrushchev, the one man who, it was said, had been able to make the grim Stalin break out into gales of laughter. Khrushchev put his talent for amusing Stalin to good use. While others were being purged by Stalin, Nikita Sergeyevich climbed the ladder of Kremlin politics steadily, rung by rung.

Of course, Khrushchev was no clown. He was the shrewd, cunning survivor of the deadly Kremlin politics that saw most of his rivals shot or ruined by Stalin. And he had a rare ability to get things done. Khrushchev, as it suited him, could play the role of moonfaced clown, showman, actor, reckless adventurer, terroristic bully or a boor who would pound his shoe on a desk at the United Nations to heckle a hostile speaker. Such a man as the head of a great superpower naturally commanded the headlines.

A master of political maneuver, Khrushchev could switch positions like a fitful breeze. When the triumvirate (which did not include him) took power after Stalin's death, Khrushchev quickly undermined Malenkov's attempt to reach a settlement with the West by attacking Malenkov's soft line—and by getting the support of the marshals of the Red Army. Then, when he had cut Malenkov down to size, Khrushchev quietly switched positions to win popularity with the Soviet people, who wanted peace. In 1957 three implacable enemies—Malenkov, Molotov, and Kaganovich—led a movement to oust him. Khrushchev teamed up with Marshal Zhukov, the head of the Red Army and the great military hero of the U.S.S.R., to oust *them* instead—not only from their positions of power in the Kremlin but even from the Communist party. A few months later, he quietly removed Zhukov from his new post of minister of defense.

Khrushchev showed an uncanny ability to survive in the game of Kremlin politics until October 14, 1964, when he was quietly shorn of power himself in a plot led by Leonid I. Brezhnev, his political disciple. Brezhnev took over the vital post of first secretary of the Communist Party, and Alexei N. Kosygin became premier of the U.S.S.R.

In the meantime, Khrushchev had dramatically changed the Soviet Union, the Cold War, and the world.

Khrushchev's career shows many contradictions. Though he had a weakness for reckless adventures and he three times brought the world to the very brink of nuclear war (twice in Berlin, and also in the Cuban missile crisis), he still staked his career on being a "man of peace."

On February 25, 1956, for example, he had shaken the Communist world with a savage denunciation of Josef Stalin before the Twentieth Congress of the Communist Party—speaking for hours on Stalin's bloody purges, his terrorism, his "cult of personality." Hardly news to the West, Khrushchev's "secret speech" (it was never published) did much to make a future dictatorship of the Stalin type impossible in the Soviet Union. The repercussions of anti-Stalinism led to the riots in Poland and revolt in Hungary that have been described. In vain did Khrushchev's detractors point out that he *must* have known about Stalin's purges. Hadn't Khrushchev personally been in charge of the Ukraine, for instance, the largest, most troubled, non-Russian republic of the U.S.S.R.? Had he not been a member of the Politburo during the terrible days of Stalin?

Before the shattering of the Stalin myth Khrushchev had climbed to supreme power in the Soviet Union—quite a distance for a man who had been born a peasant in a mud hut in the village of Kalinovka, and who spent his youth laboring in the coal mines.

On March 27, 1958, Khrushchev openly assumed the power that he had long held behind the scenes, taking over the post of premier of the Soviet Union. Almost immediately, he announced that the Soviet Union would soon overtake the United States in industrial production. That set people to scurrying around to see what the relative strength of the free world versus the Communist world really was. The recovery of both Western Europe and the Communist bloc nations had been remarkable. NATO had recovered from the scars left by the Suez crisis faster than anyone had imagined possible. Marshall Plan aid to the West and the Warsaw Pact economic cooperation among the Communist nations had proved successful. Krushchev's image as a "man of peace" lent substance to the new Soviet slogan of peaceful coexistence for economic recovery.

A new and very important factor had also come into the Cold War. On January 1, 1958, the European Common Market came into being. The original treaty nations in this daring plan for pan-European economic growth were Belgium, Italy, France, West Germany, Luxembourg, and the Netherlands. Britain refused to join. Figures compiled at the time on the economic health of the free world as against that of the Soviet bloc show the relative strength of the two thus:

Gross National Product
(All Goods and Services Produced)

Free World		Communist Bloc	
United States	$521,000,000,000	Soviet Union	$240,000,000,000
United States, Common Market, free Europe, and Japan	$881,000,000,000	Soviet Union, East European satellites, and Communist China	$416,000,000,000

Thus, in the peaceful competition of goods and services, the free world had a better than two-to-one advantage over the Soviet Union, Communist China, and the other Communist nations.

The Common Market gave an enormous spurt to Western recovery. By removing trade and investment barriers, and by encouraging the new movement of people from country to country, it played a key role in the strengthening of Western Europe.

The United States is dependent on foreign trade and depends on imports for all or part of thirty of the thirty-nine strategic minerals most vital to American industry. The United States imports all of its tin and industrial diamonds, for example, and 90 percent of its ferromanganese, platinum, mica, antimony, cobalt, and chrome and 80 percent of its bauxite, used in making aluminum. Foreign trade is vital, too, in the export of United States agricultural products and manufactured goods. Today, the United States is the largest seller of manufactured goods in the world. This free flow of goods through the world market is essential, not only to the welfare of the United States, as the world's economic leader, but to the well-being of the whole free world.

Khrushchev, dubbed "Communism's traveling salesman" by some writers, began a shrewd campaign of travels—handshaking and moving among the peoples of many nations. One of his early moves had been to journey to Belgrade to patch up the quarrel with Yugoslavia. To Britain, India, and, later, even the United States he went, acting rather like a Western county sheriff running for re-election. Nobody had ever seen such a thing before—a Soviet leader, master of the Kremlin, giving stump speeches and touring factories while visiting faraway nations!

As usual, there was shrewd common sense behind Khrushchev's travels. The Soviet leader's often heavy-handed jokes had a profound effect upon the underdeveloped nations of Asia and Africa, however much they might be scoffed at by sophisticated Westerners. Khrushchev's travels coincided with a strong economic offensive by the Communist bloc. Data compiled by the United States Information Agency between 1950 and 1960, for example, gives a clear picture of this economic offensive. The change began with the death of Stalin in 1953. Stalin, with his harsh policies inside the Soviet Union and his implacable hostility to all non-Communist nations, had had little to do with aiding anybody in a foreign nation unless the aid was given directly to Communist parties and officials who were directly subservient to him.

The new economic offensive was far more sophisticated—and effective. Khrushchev, for example, proclaimed a "vast zone of peace" made up of "peace-loving states" of the Afro-Asian areas —a prelude to Russian ventures into new areas that had been relatively free of Cold War tactics. Soviet leaders saw the less developed nations, with their weak economic and political systems, their strong nationalist sentiments and anti-colonial frustrations and resentments (mainly aimed at West Europeans) as highly susceptible to the expansion of Soviet influence. This new Soviet economic offensive, recognizing that most local Communist parties in Africa and Asia were still too weak to advance the interest of international Communism, even courted the noncommunist governments in these developing countries. The new Soviet tactics often included a temporary abandonment of local Communist party interests when they conflicted with Soviet efforts to maintain good relations with the governments in power. After Khrushchev assumed full control of the Soviet Union, the new Soviet efforts included massive aid, technical assistance, and "red-carpet treatment" of the steady parade of African leaders who were invited to visit Moscow. (A Patrice Lumumba University would later be established in Moscow for African students.) Soviet broadcasts were expanded and intensive campaigns of cultural penetration and exchanges were launched. One of the first major propaganda moves of the U.S.S.R. took place on March 31, 1958. The Soviet Union announced it had "ceased nuclear testing" and called upon the United States to do so also.

The immediate objectives of the U.S.S.R. were to foster a neutral stand by the smaller nations in East-West disputes to persuade them to side with the Communist bloc. The long-range aims were to alienate these same countries from the West and soften them up for the spread of Communism.

For a time, Khrushchev's ceaseless call for peaceful coexistence between East and West led to hopes that the Cold War might at last be coming to an end. Economic competition was, all agreed, far more sensible than rocket-rattling and threats of nuclear war that could destroy civilization.

However, dazzling Soviet space achievements and suspected Western weakness proved too great a temptation for the mercurial Khrushchev to resist. The hoped-for detente with the

Soviet Union never really came about. For on November 10, 1958, in an arm-waving speech at the Polish Embassy in Moscow, Khrushchev put aside the mask of the "man of peace" and reverted to another role in which he was expert—that of the terrorist who could cold-bloodedly threaten mankind with nuclear war to gain a political end.

The time had come, Khrushchev told visiting diplomats, for the removal of "the remnants of the occupation regime in Berlin." He demanded that the United States, Britain, and France recall their troops and to "reach agreement" with Walter Ulbricht's German Democratic Republic "if they are interested in any questions concerning Berlin." If they did not, the Soviet Prime Minister broadly hinted, another Berlin blockade might be in the offing.

In a series of speeches Khrushchev delivered an ultimatum to the West. In a note on November 27, 1958, Khrushchev made his threats official. Furthermore, he set a time limit—six months were allowed for the Berlin problem to be resolved on the Kremlin's terms.

It was, for months, a first-class war scare. The Soviet's naked ambition was to absorb West Berlin into the Communist German Democratic Republic. Secretary Dulles rejected the Soviet note the very day it was received. "We are most solemnly committed to hold West Berlin," he said, "by force if necessary." The United States would not, Dulles wrote, "enter into any agreement with the Soviet Union which, whatever the form, would have the end result of abandoning the people of West Berlin to hostile domination."

Headlines screamed of possible war. On December 14, 1958, Dulles, ill and dying of cancer, met with Britain's Foreign Secretary, Selwyn Lloyd; France's Couve de Murville; West Germany's Heinrich von Brentano; and Willy Brandt, Governing Mayor of West Berlin. They issued a ringing statement of no compromise with the Russian threats. The crisis intensified. Intricate diplomatic moves and countermoves followed. A Western proposal for a Foreign Ministers' Conference was rejected by Khrushchev, who suggested a summit conference instead.

On March 6, 1959, in a solemn nationwide TV report, President Eisenhower said that the United States would not purchase peace by forsaking Berlin. As one Western diplomat put it: "We refuse to negotiate with a pistol at our head."

Then, after leaving the world dangling for months, Khrushchev casually turned off the second Berlin crisis as abruptly as he had turned it on. In the end, Khrushchev lamely backed away from his ultimatum, saying that too much fuss had been made about the whole thing.

No one doubted that crisis would come again to Berlin. It was merely postponed until the Soviets would decide that the time was ripe because of Western weakness or disunity.

In the meantime most of America's attentions were riveted on Cuba, that beautiful Caribbean island only ninety miles south of Florida. The Cuban rebels, under the still-little-known Fidel Castro, captured most of the strategic Las Villos Province in central Cuba in late December, 1958, and took the capital city, Havana, on New Year's Day, 1959. Few dreamed at the time that one of the most gripping crises of the Cold War would one

Fidel Castro waves to crowd during his victory parade through Havana on January 8, 1959.—Wide World

day stretch from this island in the sun and reach out across the globe. Huge celebrations were held as Castro and his bearded caballeros took over after the ouster of reactionary Cuban President Fulgencio Batista. The celebrations extended into the United States—to Key West, Florida, and to New York City, where many Cuban expatriates lived. But the pro-Castro sentiments would cool rapidly as the volatile Cuban's "nationalism" came under fire from many voices both on the island and abroad. Then, on April 22, 1960, Premier Castro would charge that the United States was plotting to overthrow his government. Few paid much heed until mid-July, when Major Pedro Diaz Lans, a former Cuban Air Force officer, told a Senate Internal Security Subcommittee that he was sure Castro was a Communist. The charge startled Americans at the time. Little was guessed, however, of the deep tempests that were brewing within the American Cuban community, within America's C.I.A. (Central Intelligence Agency), and within Cuba itself.

The most startling news to the public-at-large came from the Soviet Union, when Premier Khrushchev announced that an American U-2 spy plane had been shot down over Soviet territory in May, 1960. The United States at first denied the assertion and then admitted that one of its intelligence planes had indeed been shot down. The charge and refutation, followed by the admission of the truth, led to the breaking up of the Paris summit conference as Khrushchev refused to meet with the Western leaders unless President Eisenhower publicly apologized for the incident. American prestige fell to a new low as Japan's Premier Kishi requested that Eisenhower not visit in Japan as had been planned, because of the anti-American demonstrations taking place within his country. One expert doubts that the summit meeting would really have brought the two sides together on fundamental issues anyway, especially as Eisenhower was due to be replaced in a few months by John F. Kennedy.

That summer the Cold War again shifted emphasis—this time to the huge, sprawling areas of the Belgian Congo and the neighboring Republic of the Congo on the vast African continent.

The importance to the free world of closer cooperation with Africa was especially noteworthy in this hitherto frontier area of the Cold War struggle. For the political map of Africa had changed beyond all recognition in just one decade—from 1951 to 1961. As of December 24, 1951, there were only four independent nations on that vast continent: Ethiopia, whose origins as a sovereign nation go back to antiquity; Liberia, founded in 1847 as a refuge for freed American slaves; the Republic of South Africa, founded in 1910; and Egypt.

On December 24, 1951, the former Italian colony of Libya became the fifth independent African nation. The sixth, the Sudan, was created January 1, 1956, followed closely by the independence of Morocco and Tunisia in March of that year.

Ghana and Guinea joined the parade of sovereign African states in 1957 and 1958, respectively. But the year 1960 would certainly set something of a record for Africa—or any other continent on the globe; seventeen nations were created: Cameroon; Togo; Senegal; Mali; the Malagasy Republic; the Republic of the Congo, Brazzaville and its sister Congo state, the Democratic Republic of the Congo, governed from Leopoldville—later named Kinshasa (the former Belgian Congo); Somali Republic; Dahomey; Niger; Upper Volta; the Ivory Coast; the Republic of Chad; the Central African Republic; Gabon; Nigeria; and Mauritania.

The year 1961 would see the independence of Sierra Leone and Tanganyika (now Tanzania); 1962, the independence of Uganda, Ruanda, Burundi, and Algeria.

Despite this march to statehood and independence, more than twenty territories remained under European rule, creating continuing seething resentment on the part of many African leaders. Although the United States had never been an African colonial power and had worked tirelessly with African leaders to assist them in gaining their independence, a stigma of racism had been attached to America that the Soviet Union had escaped. African leaders were much more interested in America's racial problems in Little Rock, Arkansas, and in Birmingham, Alabama, in those years than in the struggle brewing over Berlin on the European continent.

Despite these disadvantages, the West began the struggle for a free Africa with many points in its favor. African leaders have traditionally been Western-oriented by education and culture.

Ties with the Soviet Union were scant. But the U.S.S.R. had shown itself a master at troublemaking and at taking advantage of Western problems. An eruption in the Congo started the new trend toward the U.S.S.R.

Nowhere are the complex and confusing problems of the Cold War in Africa better illustrated than in the Congo, a vast 905,000-square-mile tropical jungle one-third the size of the United States.

Only by the narrowest margin was the Soviet Union prevented from acquiring a base there from which to plot subversion, infiltration, and Asian-type guerrilla warfare for all of Africa.

The problems of the Congo were, and are, enormous. All the hazards of an ill-prepared independence were glaringly apparent. The Belgian policy followed a deliberate pattern of not educating Africans above secondary-school level, and made little or no preparation of Congo leaders for independence.

As a result, when independence came in 1960, after a scant six-month interim period, few Africans had been trained to take hold of the complex task of governing the sprawling country. For instance, there was not a single native officer in the 18,000-man defense force!

On July 5, 1960, five days after independence, the Congolese Army mutinied and public authority broke down. Belgian paratroopers (who were already in the Congo) intervened to protect Belgian nationals, which infuriated extremist groups who declared it smacked of "colonialism." Then the Katanga government of Moise Tshombe seceded from the Congo. At this point, the government of President Joseph Kasavubu asked the United Nations for help in maintaining order and restoring the territorial integrity of the Congo.

United Nations forces were then sent into the Congo by Secretary-General Dag Hammarskjöld at the express invitation of the Congo leaders. When the United Nations refused to place its forces under his orders, Prime Minister Lumumba requested and received Soviet aid and assistance. At this stage, the undisciplined Congolese Army, operating without adequate supervision and control, precipitated chaos that nearly resulted in the fragmentation of the newborn nation.

When Patrice Lumumba was killed, following his dismissal as

Prime Minister, the Communist bloc, as well as a few other countries, recognized the Stanleyville regime of Antoine Gizenga as the rightful government rather than the elected government headed by President Kasavubu in Leopoldville. (The cities have since been renamed Kisangani and Kinshasa, respectively.)

The United Nations, despite this highly charged situation that could have led to a complete breakdown, was able to prevent the Communist bloc from supplying aid to Stanleyville. Its action discouraged further conflict between the warring Congolese groups and finally led to agreement between Katanga's provincial government and the central government.

The Congo's problems are still not solved, but since the departure of the United Nations forces in June, 1964, the Congolese central government has been able to establish public order and maintain the territorial integrity of the Congo. Without the earlier United Nations intervention this probably would not have been possible.

Chapter Fifteen

CRISES IN CUBA
AND BERLIN

"Ask not what your country can do for you. Ask what you can do for your country."
—John F. Kennedy,
Inaugural Address, 1961

On January 20, 1961, John Fitzgerald Kennedy, youthful (43), handsome, and very self-confident, was sworn into office as the youngest elected president of the United States, succeeding Dwight D. Eisenhower. (Theodore Roosevelt was younger, but he succeeded the assassinated William McKinley.) As his secretary of state Kennedy chose Dean Rusk, President of the Rockefeller Foundation, whom he had not met until December, 1960 —a month after his election. After a celebrated "talent hunt," Kennedy informed the press that he considered Rusk "the best man available."

Kennedy won the presidency in the closest election in American history—with a majority of only 110,000 votes out of the 70,000,000 cast. America would extend the hand of friendship, Kennedy said in his inaugural address, but would "pay any price or oppose any adversary" to preserve freedom.

The new President and his Administration were soon put to a series of brutal tests. The first, the Bay of Pigs invasion of Cuba, was already in motion when Kennedy took office.

On January 3, 1961, the United States of America severed diplomatic relations with Fidel Castro's Cuba. This move apparently took Castro by surprise. The Cuban dictator began it by abruptly ordering the United States to drastically cut the number of diplomats in its Havana embassy "within 48 hours." The outgoing Eisenhower Administration, its patience already tried by

Castro's confiscation of American property, and by his invective and other irritations, responded by breaking relations, closing its Havana embassy entirely, and ordering the Cubans to close their embassy in Washington.

This was apparently a greater reaction than Castro expected. He backtracked, but Eisenhower, who would shortly leave the White House, was adamant. The Swiss agreed to handle American diplomatic matters in Havana, and the Czechs to take care of Cuban affairs in Washington. The United States-Cuban break was made final.

Then began a dramatic chain reaction of events:

On January 5, Raul Roa, Cuba's Ambassador to the United Nations, made a charge that the American press promptly labeled ridiculous. The United States, Roa told the Security Council, was planning an "invasion" of Cuba. The C.I.A., Roa said, had set up training camps in the Central American countries of Guatemala and Honduras and was now training Cuban refugee troops for the invasion.

No one took Roa seriously then. Cuba's Ambassador to the United Nations was personally unpopular, and his excited ranting even seemed to embarrass diplomats from the more responsible Communist nations, who made a point of avoiding him. The Security Council dismissed the charge without even bothering to take a vote.

In Havana, the next day, the affair began to look like a comic opera. Castro issued a call for an all-out Cuban mobilization to repel the American invasion. Terrorists and ammunition had been air-dropped by the C.I.A., Castro shouted in a tirade that most Western newsmen found ludicrous. Tens of thousands of uniformed Cuban troops guarded white, sandy beaches or manned antiaircraft guns pointed toward blue Caribbean skies —empty of hostile aircraft. Everyone chuckled. These were more hammy theatrics by Castro, was the universal, derisive verdict.

Three and a half months passed. Castro and his United Nations Ambassador, Raul Roa, continued to make charges about an American invasion of Cuba. But they had cried wolf before, and few payed any attention. Even the Cubans grew tired of what seemed to be a charade. Most of the reservist soldiers left their antiaircraft guns and beach-guarding and went back to planting sugarcane.

Then, in the pre-dawn of April 17, came electrifying news. An anti-Castro force of Cuban exiles *had* landed on the swampy beaches of remote Las Villas Province. The principal landings were made at the Bahia De Cochines (Bay of Pigs).

Cuban refugees, brought by United States Navy ships and armed with American weapons, swarmed ashore, and para-troopers were dropped inland. United States intelligence reports had led to the hope that the Cuban people would rise up in revolt against the tyrannical Castro, and that the island would be freed from Castro's regime.

Unfortunately, aside from its diplomatic importance, as a military operation the Bay of Pigs invasion was a badly botched affair. Later, bitter recriminations would point to confusion, mis-loading of supplies, and lack of air cover as contributing to the fiasco. Castro again called for an immediate, all-out mobiliza-tion. After some initial gains by the Cuban refugees, the Castro troops counterattacked on April 18. By April 19, Castro was able to announce triumphantly that the last of the "foreign mer-cenary invasion forces" had been wiped out or taken prisoner.

The Bay of Pigs was harmful in the extreme to the United States. All through Latin America, leftist mobs staged anti-American demonstrations and riots. In the United Nations and in the world press, Castro was able to successfully trumpet dramatic charges of American imperialism.

Millions of Americans were shocked that the Central Intelli-gence Agency should have played such a role in American for-eign affairs. Others were furious that the United States, having begun the invasion, should not have carried it through success-fully. C.I.A. Director Allen Dulles, brother of late Secretary of State John Foster Dulles, ended up with much of the blame for the Bay of Pigs. After a short interval, he left office. Interestingly, the authors of this book interviewed Mr. Dulles for another book during the time the Bay of Pigs was being planned. Nothing was said about that top-secret matter, of course, but Mr. Dulles made a prophetic remark. The Central Intelligence Agency, he said, because of the nature of its secret work, can never take credit for its successes—which have been many—but its failures always are right out in the open.

Soon, Kennedy launched a much publicized ten-point, ten-year program, the Alliance For Progress, which was designed in part to stop the spread of Communism in Latin America. This program was expected to alleviate the real poverty of so much of Latin America and to provide an economic stimulus and a more proportionate share-the-wealth philosophy in the rigid, almost feudalistic societies that are so prevalent in that part of the world.

Then, too, the Bay of Pigs adventure got the new Kennedy Administration off to a humiliating start. Not the least of its legacies was the impression that the young President might be weak and uncertain. *Was* Kennedy weak? The tough and ruthless Nikita Khrushchev obviously thought so, and he devised a most brutal test for Kennedy. This time, the Cold War switched to a place of Khrushchev's choosing—exposed Berlin, 110 miles behind the Iron Curtain.

John F. Kennedy and Nikita Khrushchev held their first meeting on neutral ground—the glittering Schoenbrunn Palace outside Vienna, amid the art treasures, gilt and rococo beauty, and gardens that had once been the residence of the royal Hapsburg emperors of Austria. After a glittering round of parties and formal dinners, during which the world's press "oohed" and "aahed" over the haute couture of America's new First Lady, Jacqueline Kennedy, Khrushchev got down to the serious business for which he had come. He handed President Kennedy an *aide memoire* outlining Soviet demands on Berlin. President Kennedy read it and was shocked. He remonstrated with Khrushchev. Grimly and without a smile, the young American President remarked to the Chairman of the Soviet Union: "It looks like a cold winter."

"He didn't give an inch," Kennedy said later. "Not an inch."

The world did not have to wait until winter. The new Berlin crisis was already on.

When Khrushchev launched the new crisis over Berlin that June of 1961, Soviet military stock was very high. The Soviet space program was far ahead of the United States' and Cosmonaut Gherman Titov would soon dazzle the world further when he orbited the earth seventeen times during the height of the August crisis, many months before the United States would orbit its own first astronaut, John Glenn. This triumph in space achievements gave Russia enormous prestige. On the other hand, American military fortunes were at a low ebb following the failure of the abortive Cuban invasion. Even America's allies were gravely concerned. These factors encouraged the Russians to dust off the old threats against Berlin and try again to force the Western powers from that city.

The wily Premier Krushchev then began a campaign of terror. To Italian Premier Amintore Fanfani, Khrushchev urged that Italy leave the NATO force. He threatened that Italy could be wiped out by the Russian nuclear weapons already on firing platforms. Khrushchev then tweaked the tail of the British lion, saying: "The roar of the British lion does not terrify anyone, anymore." Not content, he then threatened the Greeks with more rocket- and nuclear-device rattling suggesting that the ages-old Acropolis could be a likely Russian target. These threats led, however, to increased unity among the North Atlantic Treaty nations to defend West Berlin at all cost. Even inside East Berlin, Khrushchev's threats set in motion events Russia had not anticipated and that it could not control.

In June, 1961, the flow of East Germans leaving their homes, families, and jobs to seek freedom in the West increased to 19,198. In July the number skyrocketed to 30,145 East German refugees as Communist-inspired stories appeared insisting that the only border still nominally open—that between East and West Berlin—should be sealed. By August 1, the hard-pressed East German economy was literally "bleeding to death" as the young and able continued to leave the country. Not since June 17, 1953, during the East German uprising, had so many refugees fled East Germany.

The grimness of the Soviet threats against Berlin became apparent to all United States citizens when on July 25, 1961, President Kennedy appealed to the American people: "We do not want to fight," he said, "but we have fought before." The President then revealed plans to step up American military preparedness by increasing the size of the Marine Corps and increasing the armed forces budget by three and a quarter billion dollars. He also announced steps to strengthen the nation's missile power and to put 50 percent of its B-52 and B-47 bombers on a ground alert that would send them on their way with fifteen minutes' warning. Draft calls would be "doubled and tripled in the coming months," Kennedy said as he announced that an increase of some 217,000 men in the armed forces would be effected.

Events moved quickly to a surprise climax, when on August 10, in the sultry heat of night, East Berlin troops marched through the quiet streets to the border between East and West Berlin and began quickly to throw up a makeshift wall between the severed halves of Germany's former capital. Barbed wire was strung to mark the division of the city. Where houses fronted on the border, doors and windows on the lower floors were sealed. Later an incredibly ugly 6-foot-high cement-block wall, topped with barbed wire and broken glass, would take the place of the hastily constructed "wall" of the night of August 10. All families living in apartments that faced on the borderline of East and West Berlin would be removed to quarters in the interior of East Berlin, and the buildings would be sealed with brick and wood, their formerly gay flower boxes left forlorn and decayed.

The building of the Berlin Wall shocked the world's conscience and again pointed up the bankruptcy of the East German regime. But the world also learned to live with its existence.

Most experts believe that it is not just control of West Berlin the Soviet Union wants. Although the Soviet Union would be delighted to see the city demilitarized—that is, by the withdrawal of the Western allies—they are realistic enough to know that this probably will not happen unless they take over by force, which could lead to total war. Much more vital to the Soviet Union is recognition for East Germany which might help prevent West Berlin's influence from undermining Communist control there. And the Soviet Union is well aware that pressure against West Berlin provides an excellent lever to try and force some form of recognition for the despotic East German state. The East German regime has been an outcast, shunned and unrecognized by an overwhelming majority of Western nations, since its birth.

The Communists know very well, of course, that full diplomatic recognition of East Germany by the West is still not even a remote possibility. During the darkest days of the 1961 Berlin crisis, President Kennedy and Secretary Rusk strongly reiterated the United States position that it had no intention of giving *de*

West Berliners try to peer over the wall dividing East and West Berlin. By November 17, 1961, when this picture was taken, the wall stood over six feet high.—United Press International

jure (legal) recognition to the despotic regime that depends upon bayonets, tanks, and the Wall to prop it up.

But there are other forms of recognition short of full *de jure* recognition. The Communist bloc would doubtless be glad to make substantial concessions even for some kind of *de facto* recognition. Nonrecognition has an unsettling effect upon the restive population of East Germany. It would be a tremendous diplomatic victory for Communism if even an implied Allied recognition of legitimacy could be conferred upon the so-called German Democratic Republic, thus officially recognizing the extension of Soviet influence into the heart of Europe.

The chances are excellent that each time the Berlin crisis flares up anew, behind the elaborate and involved Soviet legalisms, threats, and bluster, some form of increased recognition and prestige for East Germany is what the U.S.S.R. is really after.

Then, too, the Communist patience may envision a day when *all* of Berlin will be absorbed into the East German state as its capital city. To the West and to the determined West Berliners, of course, this is unthinkable.

Nineteen sixty-one drifted inconclusively on many fronts in the Cold War. Twenty thousand men and 135 million dollars were requested by United Nations forces in the Congolese civil war. In September, both the United States and the Soviet Union resumed nuclear testing. Khrushchev had already threatened the world with the Soviet intention and capability of producing a 100-megaton bomb, capable of fearsome destruction. Now it resumed atmospheric nuclear testing whereas the United States confined its tests to underground locations. An uneasy world grew more uneasy, despite the seeming lack of intensity in the Cold War.

Not until the spring of 1962 did any real action occur. Then in Laos, one of the Southeast Asian countries carved from Indochina, Cold War tensions lessened as the Soviet Union and the United States, the two major Cold War protagonists, finally reached agreement on a neutral coalition government. Since 1954, pro-Communist rebels, called the Pathet Lao, and the government troops of Laos had been fighting an indecisive but bloody war for possession of the tiny mountainous kingdom. On June 11, 1962, the agreement for a coalition government of all political forces was reached and the leaders of the factions—Princes Boun Oum, Souvanna Phouma, and Souphanouvong—signed a shaky peace agreement. While not putting a stop to all fighting, their agreement did slow the pace of escalation of the war. Sporadic raids by dissident Pathet Lao troops would continue throughout the 1960's.

Then the world found itself facing the seven most frightening days in human history.

The first public knowledge of a serious new crisis on the world scene came as President John F. Kennedy announced that a message concerning "a matter of highest national urgency" would be delivered to the American people on the night of October 21, 1962. Fifty million Americans listened, as did the world, while the President spoke of United States aerial reconnaissance planes having discovered the existence of offensive nuclear missiles and the construction of launching sites under the supervision of Russian technicians in Cuba. "Within the past week unmistakable evidence has established that a series of offensive missile sites are now in preparation," said the President. The knowledge that the nuclear warheads could travel 1,000 miles, reaching all of the United States except the far Northwest, led to Kennedy's dramatic disclosure to the American people that a "threat to the peace and security of all Americans" was involved.

The broadcast news was branded as a lie by a Soviet Union statement that the missiles were, in fact, defensive. However, this failed to alter the serious consequences of the fact that strategic nuclear devices of war had been stationed outside Soviet soil, basically altering the balance of nuclear power in the world.

Following this disclosure, the United States instituted a naval quarantine on all offensive missiles bound for Cuba and a far-reaching diplomatic effort—in the United Nations, the Organization of American States (OAS), and in every capital of the Western world—to put pressure on the Soviet Union to retreat from its dangerous adventure.

The United States gravely warned the Soviet Union that nuclear attack on any nation in the Western Hemisphere would be treated as a nuclear attack upon the United States, requiring a full retaliatory response against the Soviet Union. Both the Soviet Union and Cuban leadership responded bellicosely to the American blockade of Cuba. Premier Castro called it a violation of Cuban sovereignty and placed the island on a war footing. "Heroic defenders of the Revolution are at their posts ready to die in defense of the homeland," said Castro. Khrushchev announced defiantly that any attempt to blockade Cuba would bring on thermonuclear war.

The hastily convened OAS promptly voted unanimously to bar the importation of any missiles and urged immediate dismantling and withdrawal of the missiles already installed. At the United Nations, in a direct verbal confrontation between United States Ambassador Adlai Stevenson and Soviet Ambassador Valerian A. Zorin, Stevenson heatedly declared that the U.S.S.R. was attempting to carry the Cold War into the heart of the Americas.

The world watched as the United States blockade took effect. Troops, planes, and ships were rushed to the Caribbean, and fighter planes were poured into the small city of Key West, Florida.

"There was half an hour when we didn't know whether there was going to be another half-hour," one newsman quoted Secretary of State Dean Rusk as saying, which might have expressed best what millions anxiously feared during the height of the chilling crisis.

Finally, after appeals from United Nations Secretary-General U Thant, Khrushchev backed down. On October 28, the Soviet Premier ordered the Cuban missile sites dismantled. On October 30, the United States suspended its quarantine and the world breathed freely again. The Cuban missile crisis would later be termed the turning point in the Cold War, though Secretary Rusk would say cautiously, "I don't think we can say it was a final turning point, but everyone came away deeply sobered."

Soviet Cold War tactics, in the opinion of some experts, can be summed up in three words: "bluster and retreat." Khrushchev's aggressive rocket-rattling, the recurring Soviet-manufactured crises over Berlin, the outbreaks of guerrilla jungle warfare in Laos and Vietnam, and the Cuban missile adventure are all part of a familiar pattern of these Soviet Cold War tactics.

Ominous threats are made, the world shivers on the brink of war, then the threats or ultimatums are quietly withdrawn or

Chapter Sixteen

NUCLEAR TEST BANS AND HOT WAR IN ASIA

*"The principal problem is to organize
for peace on an enduring basis."*
—Secretary of State Dean Rusk

The Cuban missile crisis had demonstrated to the world the awesome irresponsibility of rocket- and missile-rattling and the fearsome possibility of nuclear war. The Geneva Conference on the Discontinuance of Nuclear Weapons resumed in Geneva, Switzerland, in early 1962 and showed that little had been accomplished. The last day of that conference marked the 353rd fruitless session in search of a fresh approach to the ever-present deadly and costly rivalry in the world for the possession and stockpiling of nuclear weapons. The conference had ended in failure when the Soviet Union refused to agree on an internationally controlled test ban. The West had rejected the proposed Soviet plan for self-inspection and had rejected, too, a summit meeting that had been advanced by Premier Khrushchev. "I must say frankly that I am grieved at your negative attitude to this proposal," wrote Khrushchev to President Kennedy, who shortly thereafter announced that the United States would resume underground nuclear tests.

By the time of the Foreign Ministers' Meeting in Geneva (1962) the United States, with British concurrence, had already assumed a "test and talk" policy but came up with a first plan that would ban all tests, checked by a system of national posts under the supervision of an International Control Commission consisting of four Western nations, four Communist states, and seven neutral countries. The second draft treaty would ban tests in the atmosphere, in outer space and underwater, but would not prohibit tests underground. Both proposals were rejected by the Soviet Union in 1962 but the limited test ban was accepted by them in 1963. France, a World War II ally, boycotted the disarmament talks completely. France's President Charles de Gaulle had become a highly articulate dissenter to Western alliance plans and designs. Instead, he envisioned a Grand Design with France and not the United States and Britain dominating the European community of nations.

De Gaulle had already come to the conclusion that Europe had achieved a new status as a rival to the United States, and need no longer be a dependent or a beneficiary of America. In de Gaulle's thinking, a wit once explained, a new equality among European nations, with France "more equal" than the others, came about as France began development of its own nuclear striking force.

One ray of light fell on the dismal aftermath of crisis in the Cold War conflicts between East and West. Both Western and Soviet-bloc officials unofficially predicted that by early 1963 a moratorium on testing of nuclear devices would come about.

The year 1963 brought new unrest in Asia. China was again on the move—this time in far-off mountain ranges between Tibet and India. Tibet had already been gobbled up into the Red Chinese orbit of influence. Now the Red forces struck in disputed passes between northern India and Kashmir. Although an actual invasion of Indian territory did occur and military clashes between the armies of India and China took place, the dispute ended as suddenly as it had begun. China withdrew her troops from territories she had clearly won in battle—territories previously occupied by the Indians. A cease-fire was ordered by the Chinese as a prelude to negotiations over the affair.

Not so spontaneous or so successfully aborted was the new offensive by Communist guerrillas in South Vietnam. The offensive there, led by efficiently organized groups of Viet Cong forces supplied with fine military equipment from North Vietnam, reached full-scale war proportions for the first time. President Ngo Dinh Diem's government mounted intensive military efforts, and the United States was drawn even more deeply into the quickening pace of war in Vietnam. Diem's sometime ally, France, had already announced the need for "neutralization" of

Southeast Asia and had opened diplomatic relations to Red China. The United States soon found itself involved as the major ally of the sagging South Vietnamese government. By the end of 1961, in fact, United States personnel had been involved in Vietnam combat units—though technically they were ordered not to fire unless fired upon.

Midsummer found the United States involved in a major way. "The U.S. is already involved in an undeclared war in South Vietnam," said a Communist Chinese report from Peking. Even the loyal opposition in Congress and out, the Republican Party, began to take a long look at United States involvement by mid-summer 1963. The official Republican Party publication, *Battleline,* put out by the Republican National Committee, charged that United States' rôle was "less than candid." Under fire, the United States Department of State admitted that American pilots were indeed flying combat training missions over enemy-held Vietnamese territory.

Nineteen hundred sixty-three would go down in history, however, as another major turning point in the Cold War. For on August 5, 1963, in the Grand Catherine Hall of the Kremlin's Great Palace, Soviet Foreign Minister Andrei Gromyko, British Foreign Secretary Lord Home, and United States Secretary of State Dean Rusk signed the world's first nuclear test ban treaty. Attending this historic and significant step in world cooperation were seventy United States, British, and Soviet officials. Premier Khrushchev, beaming in pride and satisfaction, also attended. All agreed that "this treaty is an important initial step toward lessening of international tension."

Premier Khrushchev called it: "An event of great international significance."

"Victory for mankind," Kennedy reported.

Later, the United States Senate consented to the treaty by a vote of 80-to-19—after debating its provisions for a scant two weeks, and the treaty was ratified by presidential signature on October 7.

That same summer of uncommon agreement and treaty-making between the sparring partners of the Cold War—the United States and the Soviet Union—saw the establishment of a "hot line" between the two world capitals, Washington and Moscow.

The direct teletype system, open 24 hours a day by a cable 4,883 miles long, would link the leaders of the two camps in the struggle for world domination. The agreement was to be called the United States–Soviet Union Hot Line Pact.

That summer saw the development of an unusual accord between the much sobered superpowers and a wrenching away from known offensives and counteroffensives in the Cold War. Many wondered if the Cold War itself had finally run its course. The outcome of the Cuban missile crisis promoted a feeling that the use of military force could not win the Cold War. For the first time, the world gave serious expression to the already developing doctrine that many of the crises of the future would not fit a Cold War equation. The disputes to come, for example, between the Greek and Turkish Cypriots, between Hindu India and Moslem Pakistan, and even between the Arab countries and Israel, would not fit into a specific pattern in the Cold War. Nor would continued upheavals of nationalism and neutralism in Africa and the broad struggle for a better life in Latin America fit the predetermined historical pattern of Cold War ideology and struggle.

By late fall, the United States would have a new president following the tragic assassination of President Kennedy on November 22. After President Kennedy died, without regaining consciousness from the brain wound inflicted by the assassin's bullet, President Lyndon B. Johnson took his oath of office. The new President, sworn into office by Federal Judge Sarah T. Hughes on the presidential plane at Dallas, Texas, repeated the oath "I do solemnly swear that I will perform the duties of the President of the United States to the best of my ability and defend, protect and preserve the Constitution of the United States. So help me God."

The new President later said, "I will do my best," and turned immediately to civil-rights programs and domestic legislation concerning tax cuts. His emphasis was definitely away from the former concepts of Cold War ideological struggles. However, the new Administration well realized that the new peaceful coexistence between the Soviet Union and the United States did not for an instant indicate that world revolution was no longer a Communist aim.

The Sino-Soviet conflicts that would again shift emphasis in the Cold War would flow from United States–U.S.S.R. peaceful coexistence. Although the developing rift between China and Russia opened over a period of time, it would be difficult to pinpoint its beginning due to the secrecy and the vague, indirect terms in which the U.S.S.R. and Red China attacked each other in public. Not until Communist China's Premier, Chou En-lai, a lifelong Marxist-Leninist, and China's Foreign Minister Chen Yi paid a visit to Albania in early 1964, did the world begin to understand the depth of the rift. The two diplomats announced to the world that tiny Albania was China's *only* European ally.

Historically speaking, the alliance between the U.S.S.R. and Red China had always been an uneasy one. The Chinese Communists, like Yugoslavia's Tito, came to power on their own, without help from the Soviet Union. Therefore, like Tito, Mao and his followers had been much less inclined to tamely accept the dictation of Moscow than such Communist leaders as Walter Ulbricht of East Germany and others in Eastern Europe, whose power depended ultimately upon Russian tanks and bayonets.

Many observers believe that after Stalin's death, Mao confidently expected to become the leading personality in the Communist world. The rise of Nikita Khrushchev had never sat well with Peking. To compound this natural antagonism, Khrushchev's blunt public criticism of Red China's commune program as an inefficient way of expanding agricultural production infuriated the Chinese Communists. Their anger was not lessened by the fact that Khrushchev proved to be right. The disasters that the Russian premier correctly predicted would result from the commune program came to pass.

Another bone of contention between Moscow and Peking is the latter's attitude toward the United States. The Red Chinese insist upon dismissing the United States in feigned contempt as a "paper tiger, entirely vulnerable to defeat." This kind of talk is known to be regarded by Moscow as dangerously irresponsible. The Russians do not want the Red Chinese to involve them recklessly in a war with the United States.

There are other, more serious differences between Moscow and Peking. Comrade Mao has little hesitation in stating that the Chinese are more orthodox Communists than the Russians. The

Red Chinese frequently charge that the U.S.S.R. has become too rich and too lacking in its zeal for world revolution.

The whole matter of coexistence is involved in this quarrel. Khrushchev had outlined a Russian program of not encouraging conflicts that could lead either to nuclear war or to wars between states. The Red Chinese contemptuously reject coexistence and profess that an armed clash between Communism and capitalism is inevitable.

Early 1964 would see the United States involved primarily in domestic problems. A flare-up in Panama seized the headlines briefly when Panamanians charged United States aggression near the Isthmus. The charge was withdrawn, however, after both nations agreed to abide by recommendations in the dispute by the Organization of American States (OAS).

In Laos, despite the Geneva coalition-government agreements that were signed in 1962, fighting was stepped up as North Vietnamese troops filed over the border on behalf of the Communist Pathet Lao forces. In South Vietnam, where the overthrow of President Ngo Dinh Diem's government and his assassination in November, 1963, had taken place, a military junta was set up. Major General Nguyen Khanh would claim that his coup d'état was aimed at stopping a French-inspired plot to neutralize South Vietnam.

President de Gaulle of France had, in fact, called for negotiations between Western nations and Communist China to neutralize all of Southeast Asia in January, 1964. "It does not appear there can be a military solution in South Vietnam," he repeated in July, and he urged an Indochina Pact to help end the fighting. United States President Johnson, however, expressed the American determination to continue to resist Communist aggression in all of Southeast Asia plus a willingness to negotiate an honorable peace.

It wasn't until the clash between two United States destroyers and several North Vietnamese PT boats in the Gulf of Tonkin off the Vietnam coast that the President urged "all out" aid. He insisted then, however, that United States policy did not consider extending the war to North Vietnam itself.

America's total involvement in the Vietnam war began at 10:39 A.M. on August 4, Washington time. It was nighttime in the Gulf of Tonkin. By radio, the United States destroyers *Maddox* and *Turner Joy* reported they were being attacked by North Vietnamese patrol boats. The *Maddox* had previously disabled North Vietnamese torpedo boats. The reports led the President and the Security Council to shunt aside the trouble brewing on Cyprus between two NATO partners, Greece and Turkey, and to re-evaluate the United States Southeast Asian policy. Later testimony (in April, 1968) revealed much confusion over the reports from the two destroyers involved in the Tonkin Gulf incident. Information was at best fragmentary. Secretary of Defense Robert McNamara acknowledged in a closed-door session before the Senate four years later that the commander of the two ships, Captain John Herrick, had sent a cable reporting that "freak weather effects and overeager sonar man may have accounted for many reports of torpedos. No actual visual sightings by *Maddox*. Suggest complete evaluation before further action."

Testimony from various officials did point out that the government had checked and rechecked the cables Captain Herrick sent verifying that torpedoes had been sighted. Several crewmen of the *Maddox* gave support to the government's decision in a television interview. An attack had, indeed, taken place, they said.

The United States Government evaluation led to plans for retaliatory attacks by the United States and the drafting of the Tonkin Resolution, later passed by Congress, "to take all necessary steps to prevent further aggression including the use of force."

President Johnson asked for radio and television time to talk to the American people that decisive August 4, 1964. He had planned to begin his talk at 9 P.M. but delayed it to give the first United States planes time to reach North Vietnamese targets. At 11:36 P.M. he spoke: "As President and Commander In Chief, it is my duty to the American people to report that renewed hostile acts against United States ships on the high seas in the Gulf of Tonkin have today required me to order the military forces of the United States to take action in reply."

As he spoke, United States planes made 64 strikes against North Vietnam, destroying 25 enemy patrol boats and nearly 10 percent of North Vietnam's petroleum storage. The change

A U.S. jet roars off the deck of its carrier in the Tonkin Gulf to raid North Vietnamese PT boat bases.—Wide World

in the character of American involvement in South Vietnam led to the cessation of Cold War stratagems in Southeast Asia as a hot, all-out war raged and engulfed the Vietnamese peninsula.

On February 7, 1965, America's bombing raids on North Vietnam began. The early raids were carried out in retaliation for a Vietcong attack on the American base at Pleiku, but by March 2, 1965, air attacks on specified targets of North Vietnamese territory to intercept the flow of men and materials moving southward from North Vietnam were a matter of military policy. America also increased its ground forces committed to battle with an enormous escalation in troops and materials. This new policy committed 400,000 American troops as against the 25,000 in Southeast Asia as of 1963.

Chapter Seventeen

PEACEFUL COEXISTENCE

*"It was rather a cessation of [cold]
war, than a beginning of peace."*
—Tacitus

If the year 1945 could be called the beginning of the Cold War, the ushering in of the year 1965 might be called the end of that conflict within the traditional and historical sense in which it had been pursued over a twenty-year period. Following World War II, the United States was forced into the vacuum created by the shattering of empires and the destruction of the balance of power around the globe. The adversary to the free world's security was the world's second power, the U.S.S.R., with its rapacious appetite for land-grabbing across the face of Eastern Europe. Almost all United States foreign policy during these early postwar years was developed from this collapse of empires and the threats presented by the Soviets. In Europe the destruction of the German power structure led to the Marshall Plan and NATO to deter Communist expansion.

But after 1950, the principal threat to world peace shifted from Europe to Asia, and again the United States was sucked into involvements there. The Korean War flowed from the breakup of the Japanese empire. The disintegration of the French and Dutch colonial holdings in Southeast Asia led to the further committment of United States resources and man-power to hold back the tide of Communist expansion. The decline of the British Empire (which had ruled much of the world and the waves for almost two centuries) to its present status of withdrawal from its farflung obligations leaves the United States the only one of the Western powers still committed to the international security arrangements for mutual defense in Southeast Asia such as CENTO and SEATO.

The early 1960's saw more changes in the traditional makeup

of the new power balances of the Cold War world. As the countries of Eastern Europe moved from satellites to something more like Soviet allies with separate ambitions, and as the Soviet Union itself moved more and more to fulfill the needs of its own people, the Soviet Communist threat to Western security continued to lessen.

Another important factor, the rise of nationalism in countless undeveloped areas of the globe, pushed the traditional Cold War responses further out of line. For with nationalism and the parade of new nations coming into being, a pluralistic world was created that no longer could be controlled and manipulated by the two superpower protagonists, the United States and the U.S.S.R. When the rising expectations of the peoples of the new nations led to instabilities, neither the United States nor the Soviet Union nor even the international organization of the United Nations could prevent these instabilities from creating new crises. Therefore, the upheavals of Israel and the Arab world, the storms in Africa, and even the struggle in Southeast Asia are perhaps beyond specific Cold War stratagems.

Despite the continuing unrest, the emergence of neutral, nationalistic nations has had a positive influence in easing conventional Cold War tensions. They have provided another bloc —of the non-aligned—which helps by diffusing and intermingling some of the stricter ideologies that mark the difference between the superpowers. This non-aligned, non-committed group of nations permits Russia and the United States to peacefully compete for their sentiments and their markets, without allowing either to dominate or control them.

Then, too, the Russia of today is a far different country than that under Josef Stalin. Peaceful coexistence would have been unthinkable between the capitalistic states and the Communist empire then. In 1953, less than a year before Stalin's death, he reaffirmed his belief that a war between capitalism and Communism continued to be inevitable.

Contrary to common belief, peaceful coexistence was not invented by Khrushchev, but by Lenin, who advocated its use by the U.S.S.R. in periods of weakness. But peaceful coexistence came into worldwide use when the Soviets revived it in the late 1950's.

It may well be that pressures have developed inside the Soviet Union that make the phrase "peaceful coexistence" somewhat more meaningful than the masters of the Kremlin may at first have intended. While the Russian attitude may still be far from what the West would hope for, the U.S.S.R.'s seeming renunciation of major force to achieve its aims appears to mark a great step forward. How reliable this renunciation of nuclear war is remains to be finally proved, of course.

Insofar as it is possible to discover public opinion inside a closed society such as the Soviet state, the desire for peace seems to be almost universal among the Russian people.

Many experts attribute this drastic change in Russian policy to the growth of conservatism inside the Soviet Union—if "conservatism" isn't too bizarre a term to apply to any Communist government.

One expert reported thus to the authors:

> The Soviet Union has been transformed from a have-not nation to a have nation. The average Russian pays lip service to the idea of world revolution, but he's much more interested in getting a bicycle, a television, a refrigerator, or an extra room in his apartment than he is in spreading world revolution. By Russian standards, the average Russian has never had it so good. The internal forces inside the Soviet Union for a peaceful adjustment of Cold War problems are enormous.
>
> There is an unmistakable decline in Russian aggressiveness in Western Europe and elsewhere where major opposition may be expected from the West. This softening of Soviet Communist aggression is a major source of contention between the U.S.S.R. and Communist China, where revolutionary ardor is still much more intense.

As early as January, 1962, an article in *Pravda,* the Soviet Union's party-line newspaper, stated flatly that peaceful coexistence had been made necessary by a "scientific and technical revolution in the military field produced by the creation of thermonuclear weapons which threaten man-kind with unprecedented losses and destruction."

The article continued:

Soviet citizens examine merchandise for sale at a government-owned store.—Sovfoto

The principle of peaceful coexistence is not a tactical maneuver on the part of the Soviet Government, as the bourgeois politicians try to present it, but a fundamental program point of the socialist state's foreign political activities. . . .

Peaceful coexistence is a dialectical process in which a most acute class struggle between socialism and capitalism combines organically with the cooperation of the states of the two opposing systems for the sake of preserving peace.

Khrushchev described coexistence as "more than the mere abscence of war, more than a temporary and unstable truce between wars; it is a coexistence of two opposing social systems, based on a mutual renunciation of recourse to war as a means of settling international disputes."

Perhaps the most candid definition of peaceful coexistence in the Russian sense was given by Radio Bulgaria:

Peaceful coexistence is . . . a new instrument for conducting class warfare in the capitalist countries and for development of national liberation movements in the colonial and independent countries.

While peaceful coexistence may have caused the leaders of the Kremlin to change the character of the Cold War, their goal continues to be the same.

"As long as capitalism and socialism exist, we cannot live in peace," Lenin declared. "In the end, one or the other will triumph. A funeral dirge will be sung either over the Soviet Republic or over world capitalism."

Khrushchev put it even more bluntly:

We will bury you. We are convinced that sooner or later capitalism will perish, just as feudalism perished earlier. The socialist nations are advancing toward Communism. History does not ask whether you want it or not!

And, lest any be misled into believing that peaceful coexistence means an end to the struggle between East and West, consider what peaceful coexistence does not mean:

It does not mean what most Americans and most peaceloving

people all over the world hope and might be misled into believing it means. It does not mean, for instance, live and let live. The basic Soviet objective, as revealed by its leaders for half a century, remains totally unchanged—worldwide Communism by any means short of nuclear war.

In this, the aims of the Red Chinese and of the Soviet Union differ. China's aim is a world dominated by Peking. In the Red Chinese means for achieving their goals, an inevitable armed conflict between capitalism and Communism is involved.

The sinister atmosphere of the aftermath of World War II brought World War II thinking to bear in new solutions for containing Communism. However, these solutions, in view of the changes afoot today, do not necessarily apply now. Perhaps the great imponderable, Red China, will provide an answer in tomorrow's world, by becoming in turn, as the Soviet Union has, a less aggressive nation.

INDEX